Don't Date Baptists

and Other Warnings
from My Alabama Mother

Don't Date Baptists

and Other Warnings
from My Alabama Mother

Terry Barr

Shawnee, Oklahoma

Don't Date Baptists and Other Warnings from My Alabama Mother © 2016 Terry Barr

Red Dirt Press
1530 N. Harrison Street #143
Shawnee, Oklahoma 74804

Cover and interior design: Smythtype Design

ISBN 13: 978-0692641200

ACKNOWLEDGMENTS: "Memories Are Made of Stuffed Cabbage" (first appeared in *The Museum of Americana*); "Over the Hot Coals" (first appeared in *Whisperings*); "Not Brand X" (first appeared in *Graze*); "Spreading The Wealth" (first appeared in *The Altar*); "Church Ladies" (first appeared in *Red Truck Review*); "Neither the Season, Nor the Time" (first appeared in *Belle Reve Literary Review*); "Searching for Higher Ground" (first appeared in *Orange Quarterly*); "Colored Memories" (first appeared in *New Plains Review*); "How Could I Tell On Another?" (first appeared in *Marathon Literary Review*); "Dead Men Don't Drink Chlorine" (first appeared in *Purple Pig Lit*); "The Mayor" (first appeared in *Rougarou*); "Classified Secrets" (first appeared in *Four Ties Lit Review*); "A Warm Place to Laugh" (first appeared in *Compose*); "In Its Infancy" (first appeared in *Blue Bonnet Review*); "But Pat Boone Never Lived in Bessemer" (first appeared in *Four Ties Lit Review*); "A View From the Seats" (first appeared in *Remarkable Doorways*); "Hey, Did You Happen to See?" (first appeared in *Turk's Head Review*); "Racial Divide" (first appeared in *Canyon Voices Literary Review*); "Star-Crossed" (first appeared in *Scissors and Spackle*)

Contents

Preface

It's true. My mother once warned me against dating Baptists. My mother is a Methodist, and I'm not sure what goes on in the rest of the country, but in Alabama, where I'm from, the Methodists and Baptists often wrestle for souls and to see who can make it first to the most popular Sunday restaurant. My mother's church, and mine for much of my early life, started services at 10:50, while the Baptists set 11:00 in stone. It's hard waiting in lines when you've just been witnessing to the lord, but it feels so good to listen to the Baptists in back of you muttering about the possibility of the restaurant running out of Greek snapper. Or turkey.

When my mother warned me against the charms of cute Baptist girls, I was fourteen or fifteen. I was a normal boy, and I know that because the first girl I ever dated was a Baptist. This, as it turned out, rather experienced young dunker let it be known though a friend that she'd welcome my advances. That happened when I was sixteen. I thought it funny even then that I, or any other healthy boy, would consider imposing a religious litmus test on any girl who would agree to, if not instigate, a date with me.

I thought it even funnier when I reconsidered the mother who issued this warning, and that the man she married, my Dad, was himself definitely not a Baptist.

He was a Jew.

Still, I didn't always ignore my mother's warnings or requests. And though she's a great talker, trained in the fine art of never letting a silence lay longer than two or three seconds, some of her words did seep in. Some, I even acted on.

Like the time she mentioned our mayor getting drunk and almost slugging a little Italian woman at a Frank Sinatra, Jr. concert.

Or the time she told our Thanksgiving table about our former neighbor next door who used to chase "the colored maids" all over the house and "bedded" many of them.

Or the time she remarked that our hometown of Bessemer was free of anti-Semitism, that is, as far as she knew.

"But Mom, just how many Jews lived in Bessemer anyway?"

Her answer was to drive me all over town pointing out the houses where Bessemer's Jewish citizenry lived. We also passed the former synagogue, which I had seen all my life but never once realized that it used to house my father's people. Her answer led me to write the history of Bessemer's Jewish life and to realize that all that I thought I knew had to be reconsidered.

In many ways, I'm still reconsidering, which is why you're reading this right now, and why I hope you'll continue reading throughout this collection.

Bessemer, Alabama, is a funny place. It's depressed, sad, violent, and maybe it's always been so. When I was a teenager, I couldn't wait to escape its confines. Eventually, of course, I did. After I wrote the history of Bessemer's Jews—including a part about my own father and his family—I returned to Bessemer with my wife and daughters to sign copies and celebrate my achievement, our achievement, with current and former Bessemerites at the Hall of History. We had a wonderful time, and the only mar to the event was that my father wasn't there. He had died just a couple of months earlier. He knew that there would be a publication; he just never got to see it.

As we left town that Sunday to return to our home in South Carolina, I felt for the first time that I was truly saying goodbye to Bessemer. I thought that it would never pull me back and that I was done letting it depress me, letting its checkered, at best, racial past anger and trouble me. Oh, I would return for Christmas visits to my mother, but otherwise, I was done. Finished.

So maybe I was the most surprised person of all when I found myself writing and publishing Creative Nonfiction about my beloved Dissie—our family maid—or about my elementary school where kids told on each other regularly and despite all obstacles, finally saw their, our, classes integrated.

Maybe I'm slow, but at some point even I caught on to the reality that Bessemer's ore was in my blood and that mining it was not going to destroy me or make me want to hide away in the Muscoda hills.

So instead of saying, as I did for so many years, that I'm from Birmingham, now I tell everyone that I'm a native of Bessemer, that town that used to have a welcome sign from the Klan on its outskirts. That town you used to have to drive through from Birmingham to New Orleans because the interstate ended just before Bessemer and began again just after it. That interstate is complete now and has been for a couple of decades at least.

So welcome to Bessemer where the Barbecue is still hickory smoked and cooked over pits; where the former synagogue still has its Hebrew letters attached and visible; and where I see Freddy and Joe, and Dissie's granddaughter Juanita every time I visit. And, of course, my mother, whose most recent words to me were not a warning, really, but a prediction: "I always said you would write a book. Now you can move on to all the others."

I dedicate this book to her and to the memory of my father, for without them, I would never have dated that Baptist girl, or wondered for so long why I shouldn't.

1
Memories Are Made of Stuffed Cabbage

My Uncle Sonny's last meal was stuffed cabbage rolls. As a guy with a very Jewish stomach, I find that strangely comforting. My Uncle Sonny wasn't even remotely Jewish. That morning he'd been transported home on the authority of his doctors who sensed the end and wanted him to exit the world on familiar ground. And he died later that night of a blood clot to the brain.

I didn't know that doctors thought such things back in 1939. Maybe they were more compassionate—more realistic about their chances of keeping a doomed patient alive. Uncle Sonny had rheumatic fever and had contracted pneumonia that week. His poor heart couldn't take the stress, and, of course, the brain clot finished him.

I can see my grandmother, in those last few hours, taking care of her only son, a college senior. My grandmother was a "doer," and she would not have stood around a kitchen table or at a bedside, fretting. She certainly would not have been immobilized by a fear of what she couldn't control. I can see the path she surely wore on the hardwood floor between the kitchen and her Sonny's bedroom. She covers him with blankets, making sure he's warm enough. She brings him water, ginger ale, anything he wants. And in doing so, she passes by my mother, who is just six years old then. Maybe my grandmother doesn't really see her little girl, focused as she is on her son who had hoped to graduate that spring.

I don't know if my grandmother had the time or presence to wonder what my mother was seeing or thinking. But I do know what my mother remembers about the last day of her brother's life:

"When he got home that day, my mother asked him what he wanted her to cook for him. Without hesitation, he said he wanted Ida Rosen to make stuffed cabbage rolls. He adored her stuffed cabbage. So my mother called Ida, who lived across the street, and she went to stuffing cabbage. He ate his last meal around 6:00 that evening."

My grandmother didn't cook much. She tended to supervise and leave the hands-on chores to my mother. My grandmother knew how to make coconut cakes, fruit cakes, fried chicken, and I see her now standing in our kitchen making sure that all the fruit is chopped just right—that the chicken is fried in proportionate amounts of Crisco. I'm sure she would have been glad to cook anything for Uncle Sonny, and I'll always wonder whether she resented him, or Ida Rosen, for depriving her of this last chance. Of course, she never told me this story—never once described to me the death of the uncle I never knew.

I also wonder if my Methodist grandmother harbored any resentment toward Ida Rosen for being Jewish. But I think this is my own worry, my own fear that my grandmother might have been a bigot. I have no evidence of this. While my grandmother faithfully gave her time to her church, she never preached the Protestant gospel at anyone. She loved her church but didn't seem to me to be particularly religious. In her waning years, she watched Sunday morning religious shows like "A Lamp Unto My Feet," rather than attending morning service. I know, too, that her favorite hymn was "How Great Thou Art," sung by Tennessee Ernie Ford.

But I don't remember her ever saying anything negative about Jewish people, my father's side of the family, or any other ethnic group. My grandmother offered her house for my parents' wedding and even agreed without opposition to having them married by a Rabbi, a stipulation insisted upon by my other grandmother who refused to attend the ceremony otherwise. To see the wedding pictures of that occasion, with everyone smiling, you'd never dream that my father's mother refused to attend all engagement parties and negotiated the wedding down to the last detail. If this bothered my mother's mother, she never let on. And she welcomed my father into her home, literally, for this is where my parents spent forty-five of the forty-eight years of their marriage.

I remind my mother of Uncle Sonny, she says. He loved movies; he kept journals; he was the first in the family to attend college—the University of Alabama in Tuscaloosa. He was a writer and a scholar—an artist and a would-be architect.

"Ida Rosen thought the world of him, too. After her daughters were born, she used to say that she wished they could have known my brother," Mom says. "It was too bad. He was so sick and the doctors really couldn't do any more for him."

I'm amazed when I think of this place and time: Bessemer, Alabama, in the 1930's. Bessemer was a mining town, a suburb of Birmingham surrounded by hills full of ore and limestone and nurtured economically by US Steel and TCI. Bessemer was dominated early on by Scotch-Irish immigrants, but if you check the city directories back in the twenties and thirties, you'll find other names—many of which you might not expect or even be able to pronounce. Names like Boackle, Koikos, Contorno, Carnaggio.

Ida Rosen's family owned *I. Rosen*, a fine clothing store on Bessemer's most elite street, Second Avenue. There were other Jewish businesses nearby, like Erlich's Department Store, Pizitz, Picard's, and up the street, The Kartus Korner. Other Jewish families in town—the Sokols, the Leftkovits, the Cherners, the Sachs, the Greens, the Becks, and the Beckers—were enough to make up two religious congregations for many years. One of these, Temple Beth-El, lasted until the late 1960's, though services were conducted by lay leaders by then. The building still stands on Sixth Avenue and Seventeenth Street. Though the Holy Faith and Apostolic Temple now meets there, the recently-uncovered Hebrew letters reveal what it used to be. I drove past the building last week as some sort of service was ending. When I was a kid, I knew that catty-cornered from the synagogue was St. Aloysius Catholic Church. I knew St. Aloysius was Catholic, too. But out of blindness or ignorance, I never saw the building diagonally across from St. Aloysius. And I don't know why.

Many of my friends attended St. Aloysius and were of Italian, Greek, and Lebanese descent. Though my father's family was Jewish, I knew little-to-nothing about the Jewish faith or culture during my early life. No one told me about Bessemer's Jewish synagogue, its Jewish life, until about fifteen years ago my mother, prompted by my question as to whether she and Dad had experienced any anti-Semitism in the city, surprised me with this knowledge. When she began listing all the Jewish family names, I was even more stunned at my own ignorance and naivety. It never occurred to me that these people were Jewish. It never occurred to me to even consider that they were Jewish. Outside of my own father and grandmother and a few other extended family members living in distant Birmingham, Jews for me were a lost, nonexistent tribe—until I left Bessemer and got far enough away to realize that the religion and culture were far richer and more widespread than I ever knew. Like so many literary Southerners, I had to leave home to appreciate the variety of my earlier life. Like so many young people who think they know their history, I had to incorporate humility into my perspective of my past.

"No, I never saw any anti-Semitism in Bessemer. People here treated the Jewish families well."

"But how many Jews were there, Mom?"

And then she showed me. We drove around, and she pointed out Jews living all up and down the neighborhoods of Bessemer. I'd never known they existed.

Today as I see the uncovered Hebrew letters of the former Jewish house of worship, I wonder if Bessemer's citizens know what they're seeing, if they ever knew. Are my mother's views on the minimal-to-non-existent anti-Semitism in Bessemer accurate? I hate to doubt her, but could she really have known what her friends and acquaintances said out of her presence? Could there really be no anti-Semitism in a city which, at least through the 1950s and maybe for a few years after, had posted along US Highway 11 (for decades, the main highway leading from Birmingham into Bessemer), a sign from the United Klans of America "welcoming" everyone to Bessemer? The sign was posted right by the ones from the Chamber of Commerce and Kiwanis Club.

In the late 1990s, I wrote an essay on Bessemer's Jewish history and interviewed many of the town's former Jewish residents. Their stories were funny and made me love and appreciate Bessemer more than I ever did. Arnold Lefkovits told of his father's winning the annual Bessemer Jaycees Christmas Light display. Jackie Becker remembered his sister's being on the cheerleading squad of Bessemer High School. Everyone I interviewed believed that here they were accepted as Jews.

I discovered some who thought that they could never get as close to their friends as they wanted. One interviewee remembered that his family wanted to move into a certain part of Bessemer, but that neighborhood had a covenant restricting Jews from living there.

Literature and histories of the Southern-Jewish experience will explain how Jewish southerners coexisted with Blacks and Whites—how the Blacks might have trusted the Jews more than they did non-Jewish Whites because the Jews were "different." As the documentary, *Delta Jews*, explains, many Jewish southerners embraced values associated with the Old Order of the South, believing that they had more in common with Christian southerners than they did with northern Jews. Which helps explain, I think, why I find this particular story so fascinating: the story of the Jewish engagement party that my mother, my grandmother, and

Miss Ida Rosen gave for Miss Ida's cousin and her Yankee-Jewish fiancée.

"So, Miss Ida calls my mother one day and tells her about this engagement party. That fifty or so New York relatives will be attending, not to mention all the Rosens from around here, and the other friends and neighbors whom she wants to invite. 'Mrs. Terry,' Ida says, 'What kind of party should I throw to welcome everyone?' So my mother thought for a minute. 'Ida, let's have a good old-fashioned Southern barbecue!'"

According to my mother—newly married herself (this was the early 1950s)—she and my grandmother began formulating the menu for this summer barbecue, which was eventually held on the grounds of the new Rosen estate on Clarendon Avenue. The mansion was a white, two-story Victorian that comprised two lots covering half of a city block.

They ran the menu by Miss Ida, who approved it all with gratitude and pride. I don't know how religious any of these Jews were. I do know that the Bessemer's synagogue was Conservative. Certainly not every Jew in town kept kosher; many attended the Reform temple in Birmingham. But for the engagement party, no dietary restrictions would be followed.

THE MENU

Iced shrimp
Cole slaw
Potato salad
Grilled chicken
Pork spare ribs
Beef brisket
Homemade peach ice cream

How you respond to this list is surely a test of whether you can be Southern and Jewish. Or at least it puts you on the road to reconciliation.

And now imagine this: a pastiche of black maids and white female socialites grilling and basting meat for hours in the hot, Alabama sun. Imagine the churning ice cream machine—hand-cranked—in the thick Alabama humidity.

"Everyone ate themselves silly, too," my mother says today, her fondness for this memory as apparent as anything I've ever heard her say. "Those Yankees ate like they had never tasted anything so good before, and you know that they hadn't either!"

A good old-fashioned Southern-Jewish barbecue, in 1950's Bessemer, Alabama, co-hosted and planned by Miss Ida Rosen and my grandmother and mother.

"And your Daddy was there too, eating ribs and ice cream and helping to clean up after!"

According to my mother, my Daddy was a welcome guest at the party. Though not a gregarious man by nature, he did possess the Southern gift of carrying on hearty conversation. And yes, he did eat pork ribs, and he ate baked ham too. He also relished a hot pastrami sandwich on rye. Born in Birmingham, Alabama, my father never shrank from being a Southerner, but then he never waved any Rebel flags either. He felt at home in Bessemer, but I think the one thing that transcended any potential problem with his Jewish-Southern identity was his dedication to and worship of the University of Alabama football team.

As much as I get pleasure from hearing this story, I know the other Bessemer, too. I grew up in the civil rights era when schools were being desegregated, when boycotts of downtown businesses, public pools, and amusement parks left all of us tense and afraid. I remember when the swimming pool at Roosevelt Park where I had taken lessons the summer before was cemented over to prevent integrated swimming. And unless you were willing to drive to a public lake some ten miles away or belonged to a private club, that meant no swimming at all during Bessemer's sweltering summers. It meant the swirling garden hose.

And yet, how does this tension and fear explain Norman Lefkovits' award for the best Christmas lights display? That a "shochet" ritually slaughtered chickens in neighborhoods on Sixth and Clarendon Avenues? That the Bright Star, a James Beard-award-winning restaurant, started by a Greek family back in 1907, still thrives today? Or that a Cedars of Lebanon club existed within fifteen driving minutes from downtown Bessemer?

Bessemer's Jews, and those in other parts of the South, were willing to remain in the public sphere during the civil rights era, but found that a small town could not hold the interest or supply enough jobs—not to mention provide enough eligible marriage partners—for the younger generation. So in the 1950s and 60s, many Jewish families moved out of Bessemer or watched their children go off to college and not return.

I wonder: at the time of this engagement party, did anyone outside the Jewish community know what was going on at the Rosen estate? That rich Jews and others were mixing religions? That if you casually drove by, you'd see white and black women serving together? I know that the Klan marched through Bessemer from time to time, but on this day, no marches occurred, no crosses were burned. It was a day of unity between Blacks and Jews in my hometown. But it was only a day. Everyone knew where they came from. When the party was over, the Yankees would go back North, the Jews would return to their enclave, the Black women would return to their side of town, and whatever had happened would become a memory.

I don't know how many who attended this celebration are still alive. Nor do I know how many told this story, and who besides my mother remembers this day. The "Bessemer Section" of *The Birmingham News* reported the event. It is archived somewhere in Birmingham's Public Library. Ancient history now, it makes me wonder at the openness of a world we usually think of as being so stratified, so closed to change. But just as I feel warm about that history, I feel the encroaching coldness of my own memory—the sense of never knowing just how extensive and rich Bessemer's Jewish history is.

I never knew my father was Jewish until I was seven years old, being driven home from school by Mrs. Shaw whose family lived down the street. I see the moment vividly.

I'm sitting in the back seat of the Shaw's '61 Ford, and Mrs. Shaw, in her seemingly sweet and even more seemingly innocuous way, turns to me and says, "Your Daddy didn't go to work today. He'll be coming home early, after temple. You know, today is the Jewish New Year."

Just like that. When I ran inside my house, I asked my mother if it was true.

"Is Daddy a Jew?"

My mother stared at me, then her gaze drifted toward and out the front screen door. As if she could still see what had just happened.

"Yes, sweetheart, your daddy is Jewish."

I didn't ask what this meant. Not then and not for several more years. But even then, I knew that I had just had a secret uncovered for me, and I wasn't sure why or what it meant.

Like many towns, Bessemer kept its secrets. And even when it acknowledged certain truths about itself, it didn't always do so publicly. Jews might be your neighbors; you just might not say so aloud.

I don't know if any Jewish families still live in Bessemer. My father died fifteen years ago. Mr. Buddy Sokol, the last Jewish man I knew of who lived in Bessemer, died just a few years later. The Beth-El cemetery between Bessemer and Hueytown will be perpetually maintained, or so I've heard. I suppose that gives me comfort. It also brings me back to my Uncle Sonny.

What made him want stuffed cabbage rolls for his last meal, and did he know that this would be his last? How did he develop such decidedly Jewish taste? Other than Ida's, we never had the dish. Not even my Dad liked stuffed cabbage, at least to my knowledge, though I also know that in my lifetime, no one ever prepared that delicacy for him. My first taste of it was at New York's Second Avenue Deli. I buy it frozen now at my local Publix market here in South Carolina, though they seem to carry it only at Passover.

Of course, someone else, when I ask for it, always prepares it for me: my mother-in-law, an Iranian immigrant. For years, I wondered how and why she knew to make this delicacy. Never a cook, she was formerly the Superintendent of Education for all of Tehran's public schools. And yet one evening, while my wife and I were visiting, she served us stuffed cabbage rolls instead of the usual Persian rice-stews. I had never had this dish before and had never tasted anything so good.

Years later, my Iranian sister-in-law announced her own discovery.

"Both of Mom's parents were Jewish. Apparently everyone knew that the Moazed family was Jewish back then, and it seems that our great-grandfather was a rabbi!"

Of course, this both explains a lot and makes me deeply happy. And without talking about what it all means or exactly which laws we might be violating, my wife, her mother, my daughters, and I continue to relish good Southern barbecued pork ribs too. In fact, I prepared two slabs for all of us last night according to the same recipe my mother's mother handed down to her.

I smile as I talk to my mother about these foodways. These memories are tinged with sadness and longing for what has passed—for all who've passed like my Uncle Sonny, a man, I'm told, I would have adored. I think now of the briny cabbage, the peppery beef mixed with onions and garlic. What a taste to remember, to savor in your last moments.

My similarity to Uncle Sonny was clear even when I was a boy. We both developed tastes beyond my Southern home. On occasion, my grandmother would look at me closely and call me to her side. In her last years, I know that her memory was at times clouded, though she never totally lost her presence of mind. She'd call out to me and I'd come. Like everyone else in the family, she referred to me as "Buddy." But I'd come to her even when she saw someone else. Even when she called me "Sonny."

2
Over the Hot Coals

In Memphis once for a meeting of the Southern Jewish Historical Society, I joined my other faithful Hebrew attendees for an evening on Beale Street. Seated at BB King's Blues Joint for supper, the twenty of us were given the choice of a barbecue pork plate with slaw and beans, or the fried catfish platter.

It was a funny moment, and you might imagine that the Rogoffs and Cohens and Weiners and Barrs at the adjoining tables felt out of place. Given the menu options, you might also imagine that our individual and collective faces wore looks ranging from dismay to disgust. But actually, only one of the diners asked for a vegetarian plate. The others, including the daughter of a well-known Birmingham rabbi, made their choices lustfully, the only real instant of distress being how to choose between two such scrumptious Memphis-Southern delicacies.

The rabbi's daughter ordered the pork plate and I chose the catfish. The catfish tasted mighty fine, fried crispy golden-brown, the crust insuring that the sweet moisture of that bottom feeder exploded in my mouth. As good as the fish was, though, I looked at the barbecue pork with total longing and envy. I wasn't eating red meat then; neither at that time was I gluten-free. Times change, however, and we learn to adapt.

I now fry catfish after I've rolled it in gluten-free breading.

More importantly, though I feel politically incorrect and ask for mercy from my liberal-Jewish gods, I once again eat pork. Pork cooked over hickory wood fires. Pork smothered in fiery red sauce. And since I'm really only half-Jewish, but all Southern, I no longer feel alien in the region I call home. In fact, my newfound, or rather newly rediscovered love of barbecue helps me recall a past when barbecue pits and hickory wood coals were as much a part of our sacred home ground as our fertile pecan trees and earthy red clay.

A time when "Let's have a Barbecue" didn't mean switching on a gas grill and burning a few burgers. For in my time, a "Barbecue" meant an all-day celebration with a community. A homogenized community with its own flair and flavor and amenable quirks.

My mother never needed a reason to barbecue. As she tells it, from the time she was a girl, the grocery stores in Bessemer, our Alabama hometown, all closed on Wednesday afternoons. So most of the neighbors on Fairfax Avenue—my mother's family, the Colquitts, the Staubs, and the Battons who all lived across the street—would barbecue together on those summer Wednesday evenings. Barbecues aided and tended by the various maids in the neighborhood's employ. It was at one of these Wednesday rib suppers that the Batton's daughter Margaret met a young man who had just bought a house on the next street over—a guy who had served his country in World War II, losing his twin brother during that conflict, and who was now trying to live out his American Dream back home: Joe Terry. Eventually Joe and Margaret married, and then bought and moved into the Staub's house right next to Margaret's parents. Over the ensuing years, those Wednesday feasts became reduced and ritualized into only Fourth of July and

Labor Day barbecues. The attendees shrank as well, so that by the mid-1950's, just the Terrys, Battons, and my mother's family, which after 1952 included my father, celebrated these occasions with basted pork.

In my memory, when my family hosted the event, the Terry family actually invaded. There were nine of them at least, and only five of us at most. We'd set up picnic tables in the back yard, just a few feet away from our grill, which, even though it stood four feet tall, we always referred to as the "barbecue pit." To call it either a grill or a pit doesn't do it justice though, or maybe I should say that our contraption could not do justice to the terms "grill" or "pit." For what we had was a black and round and not very deep metal contraption that no doubt one of my parents bought at the local Rexall Drugs. I can still see the burning and later completely white-ash Chuck Wagon charcoal briquettes, in the shape of wagon wheels. When they finally cooled, I always hoped I could pick one up whole and keep in intact. Obviously I couldn't, but in that hope lay something deeper, though of course it would take me decades to appreciate this yearning.

In my family besides my mother and father were my mother's mother, "Nanny," and my little brother Mike. The Terry family consisted of the parents, Joe and Margaret, Margaret's parents, the Battons, whom the grandkids referred to as "Mom" and "Pop," and the five kids: Jon, Joe, Mary Jane, Margaret Lou, and Jack. In my earliest memories, Jack hadn't been born; in fact, when Margaret became pregnant with him, everyone was surprised, not least of whom Margaret and her husband Joe themselves. For Jack was born some six years after the former youngest child Margaret Lou, and whether he was actually planned or not, he still received a name beginning with a "J" to match his brothers and father, the girls' names starting with an "M" to honor their mother. I don't know if that naming habit seems strange now or not. What I do know is that I knew no other family then, and certainly none now, quite like these Terry's.

What I mean by that is that in our household there was an

obsessive-compulsive sense of order. Our mealtimes, bedtimes, waking up times were all rigid and regulated. My father had a routine he followed every day of his life from his morning calisthenics to his driving route to work, favorite push-button-programmed radio station, and nightly TV viewing schedule. On weekends he cut the grass whether it needed it or not, raked leaves systematically and completely, and then hollered the next day when more leaves, just to frustrate him, decided to rain down on his pristine yard. He took us to see his mother every Sunday, same time, same take out deli food, and if I asked to take a different route, say through downtown Birmingham, I did so at the risk of being scolded or even shouted at for causing trouble. Some evenings he relented and humored me, and I like to think that when he saw the lights of the theater marquees in downtown Birmingham, he enjoyed the spectacle as much as I did.

My mother or our maid Dissie vacuumed the house always on Mondays, Wednesdays, and Fridays. Grocery store shopping was a regular Friday morning affair. Mom had her "Sprig and Twig" Garden club and Alethian Club on alternating Thursdays, her Bridge Club on Tuesdays. Each weeknight supper was also set and recorded: Monday, leftover roast beef from Sunday lunch made into hash, or leftover leg of lamb covered in barbecue sauce; Tuesday, veal cutlets with a side dish of Franco-American spaghetti; Wednesday, fried chicken; Thursday, grilled steak and baked potatoes; Friday, vegetable soup or chili. In the grocery store, she traveled the same patterned aisles, and each night she always had my brother and me in the bathtub by 7:30, and in bed by 8:30.

So maybe we were a peculiar family too, but at least you could count on us to be where we were supposed to be: at clubs, at work, at the table, or in bed.

Not so the Terry's.

Their children did have regular after-school activities: ballet, boy scouts, piano and speech lessons; Girls' auxiliary at the church. Mary Jane was my age, a mere two months older, and as little kids, we played together all the time, making mud pies and playing hop scotch and rock school. But when she turned six, her after-school afternoons were booked solid, and it felt like I hardly saw her at all, which was too bad because in those years, she was my favorite friend. We became boy and girl-friend in fifth grade, a "relationship" that lasted exactly one year, though the most we ever did to consummate that affair was square dance as partners and ride our bikes under the same oak tree full of mistletoe.

But while the Terry children had outside activities, which did wield some sense of order, at home, in all the odd hours between activities, you could see and hear the chaos unfolding. The two houses—the Terry's and next to it the Batton's—functioned as one. When I'd be playing in the front yard, the traffic between the houses always caught my eye. Sometimes I envied them, having two places to use as command posts for various war games, but then I'd hear, and I'd see the trouble.

Margaret Terry would appear on the front steps or in between houses and start screaming for one of the kids. But if she started out yelling for Jon, she always and forever included them all, rattling off their names in one synchronized wail: JONJOEMARY-JANEMARGARETLOUJACK. Even before Jack was born, it seems to me now, she included his name in the yelling. From my yard I could see several Terry kids hiding around corners, in boxwood bushes, up trees, anywhere to escape their mother's fury. It wouldn't matter what they had done or were supposed to do, either. The longer she yelled, the LOUDER she screamed, the worse things ended up being. When they approached near enough, never really anxious but usually like a stray dog who wants some attention but isn't quite sure he'll like the kind he's about to get, she'd start chasing them, slapping old clothes at them, trying to grab their collars or necks, so as to "switch" their butts till they promised to behave which, if they ever did promise, they broke just as soon as they got back out of doors again the next day or even, as they got older, that very night.

I know the Terry's ate supper. I just don't know when or how or who ate together. I wonder if they ever ate together. I'd be invited for lunch on occasion, maybe for a bologna or tuna sandwich. But in the chaos dreams of these memories, mainly I see Mary Jane and Margaret Lou and Joe at our house, enjoying my mother's cooking and only departing reluctantly from our order to their anarchy.

And yet, when our house caught on fire during the middle of a frigid January night, it was to the Terry's we turned. They provided for us willingly, warmly. I remember bedding down on their living room couch that fiery night. I was only five, not sure really what had happened, what it all meant, how my world would ever be the same, but in the morning, waking up in a safe place, a place I knew, with the assurance that all would be OK. After all, Mr. Terry, or "Big Joe," was our Safeco insurance agent, taking care of both our refurbished home and all of our cars.

Throughout my public school life, our families carpooled together to school, our parents trading off the days or weeks of chauffeuring. And through my college years, we barbecued on those two summer holidays faithfully, though the meals and those attending them finally grew old and much too thin.

In my earliest memories what the elders barbecued most and best were ribs. I didn't know then how long and intricate and tiresome the process of cooking ribs is. That is, if you do it right. All I knew was how good they tasted. You couldn't get me to eat potato salad or baked beans, so as a five or six-year old, I'd receive three or four ribs, separated for me by one of my parents, and I'd grab a few chips and maybe some slaw. This was Alabama, so of course the rib sauce was homemade and ketchup-based. I learned the sauce recipe when I went off on my own, but what I really learned about it is that the recipe is instinctual, meaning that my mother—or any other proper chef—can tell you the ingredients, but the amounts, you have to figure more or less on your own, understanding the distinction between "a little bit" and "some,"

or " a teaspoon" from "several drops." And of course, the amount varies with the number of slabs of ribs you're cooking. Back then, with fourteen-plus people, six slabs would be about right. And back then, the ribs were the big kind, spare ribs, though today my mother gets incensed if you, or any barbecue establishment, use anything but St. Louis style or Baby Back ribs.

"They're more tender, just better," she insists.

Stupidly—for over these decades if I've learned anything it should be not to question her culinary skills and experience—I cooked some spare ribs last summer. Everyone ate them, but I didn't get the rave reviews I usually do. My daughters, my biggest fans, were particularly silent, and I noticed uneaten ribs on their plate and too many leftovers. So a month or so later, I bought some Baby Backs. Two slabs for five people. Those ribs didn't "make it through the night," making me proud and making the echoes of Kris Kristofferson even more woebegone.

So for years, the Terry-Batton-Barr Labor Day/Fourth of July barbecues were rib-based. Then, and I'm sure this depends entirely on who you ask, which family group that is, Miz Batton, "Goldie" to her dearest friends, decided to barbecue a Boston Butt. Not that there's anything wrong with a Butt; it makes a fine sandwich when slow-cooked to its most tender, moist best. But the bread interferes and it doesn't have the chewy, gnaw-the-bone immediacy. Somehow with ribs, the flavor and the hickory smoke resonate longer and you want to eat more and more. And of course, you can even when you're five or six because elders love to see a growing boy eat.

So for a few years, the Batton-Terrys would serve Butt and we would serve ribs, and it might have been the seeming price inequity or just the tiresomeness of cooking and basting and turning those ribs every half-hour on such a small BBQ pit, but one year we served a Butt too.

And one year, after Miz Batton grew too old to administer the cooking, Big Joe took over, and once, when he carved his Butt, blood sort of oozed out, and my mother said to us, "We're not eating any of that." I don't remember what we did then except fill our plates with beans and slaw and potato salad, which, by then, I was eating with relish.

There was another year, too, when Miz Batton forgot to put sugar in the homemade vanilla ice cream.

"Goldie," her husband exclaimed, "there isn't a grain of sugar in this ice cream!"

"Why there most certainly is," Goldie shot back.

But there wasn't, though according to my Daddy, that didn't stop Big Joe from eating a heaping bowl full.

So our backyard barbecue fests weren't always flawless.

But after those suppers, we kids made them even more special with our nighttime games of "Hide and go seek" and "Ain't no boogers out tonight." I kept thinking in the year that Mary Jane was my girlfriend that on one of these holiday nights, I might catch her for a kiss. But that never happened, another in my series of dream-regrets.

As the years passed, the older kids would bring girl and boy friends. And then the time came when one or two quit coming, either being off at school or invited to a boy/girl friend's house. And one year we went across the street to the Terry's to find Mary Jane's boyfriend Bill watching over the grill.

"Check this out," and by his tone, we knew we were in for something, just not something good.

He opened the grill lid, and it wasn't ribs and it wasn't even a Butt.

It was a ham.

Barbecued ham.

And off to the side were some vinegar-basted chicken quarters. Now I know I sound spoiled and picky, but that's where the biannual neighborhood feasts died for me. I'm sure many there ate the ham. I have come to understand that in certain regions of the South, Jackson, Georgia, for instance, uncured hams are thrown on the pit and then cooked and chopped to the grill-master's preference [see Robb Walsh's *Barbecue Crossroads* for more information on this and other treats]. But the ham on Joe Terry's pit was a very pink picnic cut. I couldn't eat it, and I'm not planning on hitting Jackson, Georgia, anytime soon either.

I know it sounds like I'm blaming our good friends and neighbors for changing our practices, and in a way, that *is* what I'm doing. But I'm not mad, sad, or hurt. I think everyone did their best whether they slaved or just ate, forgot the sugar or ran errands, left the supper much-too-early, or decided that they could spend only so much cash.

It was our community. And our barbecue tradition spanned some forty years while our neighborhood's "old south" ways remained intact.

At my last barbecue with the families—and by this time, all the grandparents except Miz Batton had passed on—the only "kids" left were me and Mike, Margraet Lou, and Jack. At the end of this Labor Day meal, Big Joe and my Daddy drove me the fifty-mile round trip back to college. They talked the way down about business and Alabama football. They didn't share old memories of past barbecues because that wasn't quite their nature, and besides, I'm sure neither thought this would be the end.

But it was.

Today in my home in upstate South Carolina, we still barbecue at our house, often inviting friends and neighbors to join us. But there's nothing regular about these gatherings and nothing ritualistic either, except how I marinate and baste and barbecue those Baby Backs or St. Louis ribs, the only meat I ever take the time or care to cook on the old charcoal and hickory grill we've used for almost fifteen years, after buying it second-hand from neighbors who were moving away.

This kind of eating probably isn't so healthy and it certainly isn't kosher. But it's a part of me, just like my name: Terry Barr, and while there have always been unanswered questions about whether our branch of the Terry's (my mother's family name) is kin to their branch, what I can say is that "Little Joe" Terry and I remain in contact through several states and over all these years. He tells me that from time to time he drives through our old neighborhood too. Neither of our families has lived there since the mid-1990's.

"It's sad," he says. "The whole street has just gone down. I wouldn't advise going back there."

And mainly I listen to him. But I did drive past our old houses once, even driving through the alley behind our house where I could still see the scenes of those long-ago barbecues. I wish I hadn't, though, because I saw other things: the reality of what we felt like we had to escape.

I saw that it wasn't only my memory that had faded a bit.

But I suppose that's the price we pay when we give up our old homes out of fear of what is new and different. When we quit barbecuing with our neighbors because they no longer look like us or talk like us, though if we had taken the time to study ourselves more closely, we might have learned that, in the end, we all love our ribs with red sauce cooked over a pit of hickory wood.

For we all are, finally, true products of a culture whose embers will never completely die.

3
Not Brand X

My family displayed loyalty in a variety of ways: to each oth-er; to weekly TV series like "Combat!" or "Perry Mason;" and perhaps most importantly, to food. And when I say "food," I don't mean simply choosing ground chuck over regular ground beef, or using strictly white corn for creaming and yellow for gnawing off the cob, though none of us would have chosen or dared to do differently. I mean brands: brand loyalty.

For instance, my Dad swore that only a simpleton would choose Keebler or Sunshine cookies over Nabisco. His one excep-tion to this rule was Sunshine's "Vienna Fingers."

"They're much better than 'Cameos,'" he'd say, referring to Nabisco's brand of cylindrical vanilla sandwich cookie. But if you offered him a "Hydrox" instead of an "Oreo," or if my brother and I talked our Mom into buying Keebler's feeble substitute for "Chips Ahoy," then we'd all get a twenty-minute dissertation on quality, freshness, and flavor, and most energetically, loyalty.

"We're a Nabisco family. Don't forget it!"

Of course, none of us could forget it, and though I don't eat "store-bought" cookies today (except for the gluten-free oat-meal-raisin variety produced by Whole Foods), if I were to violate my code of digestion, I'd buy Nabisco; I wouldn't think of straying even though my Dad has been dead for fifteen years.

It's not just cookies; it's everything food-related.

I've long passed the point where I smear ketchup on meat. Ok, sometimes I sneak it on a few French fries, for nothing weds deep-saturated potatoes and oil better than a sugary red concoction that drips from an iconic bottle. Today, instead of ketchup, I prefer hot sauce on burgers and hot mustard on kosher dogs. And I'd definitely never pour ketchup over fresh fried shrimp or fish, for I remember watching my brother be severely scolded by the manager of one of Birmingham's finest Greek eateries when he foolishly spread his ketchup over a piece of fried red snapper. You might wonder why this culinary palace served ketchup at all. I don't know. Why do people order Diet Coke to go with their three-piece KFC meal—the one with "mashed" potatoes, gravy, and all those rolls or biscuits?

But if I were to use ketchup, the only ketchup I'd consider buying—and if you know the distinction in the terms "Ketchup" and "Catsup," you'll know where I'm heading—is Heinz.

All because of Dad.

"Stokely's is too runny, and Hunt's just doesn't taste as good. Besides, who wants something called Catsup?"

I mean, you could try to engage with him in this argument, but you wouldn't win. Just as Woody Allen lamented that his fictional parents in *Annie Hall* would argue over which was the greater ocean, the Atlantic or Pacific, my Dad would willingly engage in any argument over, and indeed always have the last word, in ketchup. He wouldn't eat Chinese food largely because he couldn't decide where the Heinz should go. So whether I use it or not, whether I need it or not, in my pantry right now is a bottle of Heinz. If, two or three years from now, I run out, I'll buy another at our local grocer's.

Another bottle of Heinz.

In fact, just last week I made a meat loaf for my Persian mother-in-law. I added a local barbecue sauce to the insides, but at the end, I topped it with Heinz. She and everybody else loved the meat loaf. And somewhere, I know my Dad is smiling.

My Dad, however, was just that first ingredient in our family's brand-loyalty layer cake. He never cooked—except the occasional French toast for breakfast—so he had no idea of the proper ingredients for sauces, for desserts, for baking. That was my Mom's province, and as a southern cook with ties to several generations of home chefs, she experimented with, decided on, and served up meals that are still talked about among her peers and mine.

The only brand food that Dad ever questioned her about was mayonnaise. According to Mom, you're just a fool if you use any mayonnaise other than Hellman's or Kraft. And even with Kraft, she'll sigh and wonder just a bit about the universe your ancestors abandoned to get here. Every now and then, and I believe he did it just to make her pressure rise, Dad would claim that Blue Plate or Bama tasted better. It's funny that he would brook no dissent on ketchup, yet he egged mayonnaise on her:

"Blue Plate? Echhh. You just don't know what's good!"

And he'd just laugh and walk away.

Remember, we're talking about mayonnaise, not Miracle Whip or Smart Balance. But before you ask, "Who really cares," query your friends and in-laws. I bet most have an opinion, and many will go to war over their favorite. For years, my in-laws bought Kroger brand, but then, they weren't from "here."

Recently, having lived in South Carolina these past twenty-seven years, I bought my first jar of our locally manufactured mayonnaise, Duke's. But I'll never do that again. I keep finding ways to use masses of it in tuna or turkey casseroles that I prepare for other people. From now on, it's Hellman's or nothing.

Aside from mayo, my Mom's loyal favorites run the spectrum from flour—only White Lily—to cornmeal—only Jim Dandy. From canned tomato soup—Amy's Chunky Tomato Bisque—to chocolate syrup—definitely only Hershey's. And if you want an eighty-two year old woman to switch your legs, please don't ever suggest that she have a Pepsi.

I rarely run afoul of Mom when it comes to her favorite brands, except for the time when I found myself trapped between grocer and mother. The time when I just didn't understand that when my mother told me what to buy, she wasn't giving me free will.

Understand: there is no free will when it comes to baking powder. There can't be.

For only a simpleton, or a five year-old boy, would bring home anything other than Rumford Baking Powder for his mother's angel biscuits.

"Buddy! Run down to Lorino's and get me a can of Rumford Baking Powder. I need it for the biscuits I'm making tonight. That's Rumford, you hear!" and she even wrote it out for me on the back of an index card.

"Here's a dollar. That should be enough."

Lorino's was an old-style corner grocery at the foot of 19th Street, just a block-and-a-half from our house. It was one of those stores where the owners, if they wanted, could live in the back, as it faced 19th, but extended down Exeter Avenue with a separate entrance at the rear. The Lorinos were ancient to me even then, and I don't know how long their store had been operating. Their son was a star running back for Auburn in the 1950's, and his photo adorned the wall just behind the counter.

I thought Lorino's was good for buying cold Cokes from the floor cooler and oatmeal cookies from the enormous glass jar sitting by the cash register. But Lorino's was also disappointing in that while they sold any variety of bubblegum you wanted—Bazooka, Double Bubble—they never carried bubblegum cards. Not baseball, football, Beatles, Monkees, anything. Every time

I entered, I looked longingly at the rows of candy and treats on display just behind the counter, and once, I thought I spied a glittering pack of football cards. But no. It was just a "WOWEE Whistle," an orange, wax, and I think edible device to blow shrilly on and drive your parents crazy during Halloween season.

So the treats at Lorino's were just as limited as the atmosphere.

As I remember it now, the large plate-glass window out front afforded most of their lighting. Surely, though, there were overhead lights in the store, and maybe they were fluorescent, but Lorino's just didn't seem that bright inside. And the floors were not polished linoleum, but rather hard stone, concrete, and a dirty euchre color.

The fact of it was that Lorino's was one of those stores that presaged 7-Eleven's and Quik Marts; where kids walking home from school bought their treats; where people like my Mom would run in if they needed one or two items that they had forgotten at the supermarket; and where the bifurcated white and black neighborhoods of our small Alabama town met, as 19th Street was the general segregating line on this side of Bessemer. Only those without cars would have done major grocery shopping there. But then those without cars back in this era would never have been able to afford much, would never have bought much. Could Lorino's have made any sort of profit, or were the rumors true that the Lorinos were propped up in this enterprise by those who persuaded them to move into this store—those who wanted their son to play football for Bessemer High?

Of course, I didn't know any of these stories then. For me, any chance to go to Lorino's was thrilling, especially if I were being trusted with an errand for my mother. So on that day of the baking powder excursion, I pocketed her index card and dollar bill, buttoned my jacket, and headed out the back way, down our pecan-tree lined backyard, across the alley, and over to the corner where Lorino's sat.

Opening the screen-door entrance, I walked hesitantly up to the counter. Rather than falsely describing Mr. and Mrs. Lorino, since my memory of their faces has disappeared, I'll simply suggest that you picture a generic Italian, Mom and Pop couple in their seventies: short, somewhat squat, very gray. And hairy. Overall, they were friendly enough, and maybe it's just my imagination now, but whenever a kid or several kids entered, the Lorinos would huddle together, as if only in unity would they be able to fend off, or sell canned goods to, these threatening vagrants.

"Can I help you," Mr. Lorino asked, as if he knew he couldn't.

And in a voice that somehow knew that this experience was more doomed than not, I said,

"Could I have a can of Rumford Baking Powder please?"

I don't know how to describe the look of pure horror that passed over his face. It was equal to what I imagine he'd have expressed had I asked instead, "Would you mind if I steal a few cookies and bring in an older gang to help me?" In his shock, or dismay, or abject fear at my request, he must have covertly motioned for Mrs. Lorino to move closer to him. I never saw him make the motion, but in an instant, she did so. Putting his arm around her, protecting all that he held dear and safe, he said, not apologetically, but almost threateningly,

"We don't carry that brand. All we sell is Calumet."

Calumet brand, like Rumford, was also baking powder and it also came in a red can. Only Calumet had an Indian on it, though I had no idea why. In any case, I surely didn't expect this trouble. Maybe I had wondered beforehand if I had enough money, if I would lose the money on the way, or if I would even lose the index card. But I never figured that Lorino's wouldn't have the brand I needed.

The brand my mother depended on.

So with the two old people staring at me so intently, as though if I didn't make a decision fast they were going to exercise some privilege only known to small Italian shopkeepers living in Bessemer, I blurted out what came first to my mind,

"OK. I'll take that one."

Mr. Lorino proceeded to put the Calumet in a small brown

sack, took my money—I did have enough—gave me back a nickel change, and sent me on my way home, thinking I had made the best and only decision I could have made.

Even now, I wonder what other decision a boy like me could have made: "No thanks, we only use Rumford?" "I'll have to think about it?" "Could I use your phone?" Maybe other five year-olds would have been more thoughtful, more discerning, more inventive. But not me.

I picked up my bag and went straight home. I didn't walk past the creek that ran beside Lorino's, nor did I amble by the TVA power station, dreaming of the warning I had always been given to never think of touching even the outside fence for fear of being electrocuted.

But being electrocuted couldn't have been much worse; in fact I think it would have been remarkably similar to what I experienced when I entered the kitchen where Mom was stationing all her biscuit-making equipment. Pulling the can of Calumet out of the sack, I stood it on the counter, right next to her mixing bowl.

"What is this? This isn't Rumford! What have you done?"

"They didn't have Rumford. This was all they had. I didn't know what else to do."

"Well...."

Here you might think my mother was about to soften, to tell me that it was all right, that I did my best. With a pat on my head, she would acknowledge that in unforeseen circumstances, making such a weighty decision was too much for a five year-old anyway.

But that wasn't my mother, and since you don't know her, you'll have to trust me when I report that instead of the forgiving, reconciling scene above, what followed her "Well," went pretty much like this:

"...you're going to have to take this back and get my money. This stuff is no good at all. It makes food bitter. I don't want my biscuits turning out bitter. I only use Rumford. Now march down there and take this mess back right now!"

I must have gone, though if I did, I ghost-walked the Calumet to Lorino's. I suppose that my mother went to the supermarket later, or maybe she borrowed the heaping teaspoonful of Rumford from one of our neighbors. But what I do know is that I never entered Lorino's again without thinking of Calumet Baking Powder which, to this day, I've never purchased again, though I'm sure I've eaten it in baked goods since.

None, of course, from the hands of my mother.

On those occasions when a piece of challah or cornbread or angel biscuit leaves a bitter taste in my mouth, whether it's true or not, fair or not, I think one thing: Calumet. Ugh.

In composing this story, I asked my mother to help verify the details. She did so, but thinking of the incident, of the Calumet, just got her stirred up again.

"I don't know why people can't taste the difference either. Why, my family has been using Rumford for generations. My mother and my Aunt Ann. When I was a little girl, no more than five or six, my mother took me to a friend's house for lunch. The food was pretty good, but not the biscuits. When we were on the way home, I asked my mother why the biscuits tasted so bad. 'It's the baking powder,' she said. 'That bitter baking powder. They didn't use Rumford!'"

My grandmother went on to explain that there were two kinds of baking powder: phosphate, like Rumford, and tartrate. Like Calumet.

"You just have to be a cook to know the difference," Mom said. "I've never forgotten that day either!"

And now, neither will I.

As I rummaged through my mother's pantry, conducting my research, I found her can of Rumford. She has no one much to bake for these days, as we all live hundreds of miles away. Maybe that explains why her can of Rumford was dated June 1999. In any case, she purchased it while Rumford still owned its own brand, based in Terre Haute, Indiana. On that can, Rumford, as if it were channeling my mother and grandmother (and even Aunt Ann) instructs:

"Use double acting Rumford Baking Powder in the exact

quantities called for in your favorite recipes. Rumford is an all-phosphate baking powder—this is your assurance against any bitter after-taste."

When I went to our local Publix Market, I explored further. Rumford is now owned by Clabber Girl, another brand of baking powder my mother disparages. I examined the ingredients of both brands and saw that there are two main distinctions: first, Clabber Girl contains aluminum (as does Calumet by the way); second, Rumford's powder is certified non-genetically modified organic, something my old-styled mother could care less about. Neither Clabber Girl nor Calumet makes that claim. And while all claim to be gluten-free, it is easy to see that Rumford costs roughly twice as much as the other two. Which is also part of my family's history of food-brand loyalty. "You pay for what you get," my mother has always said. So true.

And another thing I know: as I continue to pass on my own foodways to my daughters, as I give them recipes in my own hand that call for certain ingredients, I always specify the brand: Crystal, Heinz, White Lily, and of course, Rumford. For my best and only intention is to leave a sweet taste in their mouths and in all of our memories.

JO ANN'S ANGEL BISCUITS

5 cups sifted flour (White Lily, of course)
3 tsp **RUMFORD** baking powder
1 tsp baking soda (Arm & Hammer)
2 tsp salt (Morton's)
1 pkg yeast (Fleischman's)
1½ cups buttermilk (Barber's in Birmingham)
¼ cup sugar (Dixie Crystals, though I won't complain if you opt for Domino)
1 cup shortening (Crisco)
2 Tblsp warm water (tap)
    1. Sift dry ingredients and cut in shortening.

2. Dissolve yeast in warm water, then add buttermilk.

3. Add buttermilk and yeast mixture to dry ingredients. Mix well.

4. Place dough in refrigerator (Frigidaire).

5. When ready to use, roll out dough and bake as needed at 450 degrees for 10–12 minutes.

4
Spreading the Wealth

On a one-mile stretch of highway leading from Bessemer, Alabama's iconic barbecue restaurant, "Bob Sykes," to the entrance of the decades-defunct West Lake Mall, there are roughly fifteen establishments providing consumers with seemingly free money. While their names vary—"Title Loans," "Cash for Gold," "E-Z Cash," "Checks Cashed, No Questions"—the aim is the same. Quick money. With strings.

If a community's most popular form of commercial enterprise is making money off of lending money, the end must be in sight.

I grew up in Bessemer, but for the past twenty-seven years I've called Greenville, South Carolina, my home. The tall corporate bank buildings dominate its skyline, promising and actualizing the lending/investing of capital, and have resurged a downtown area that is now the envy of medium-sized cities across the country. Greenville regularly finds itself mentioned in magazines such as *Southern Living* and *Garden and Gun*, and recently it made *Time Magazine*'s top ten cities that have turned their downward-sloping fortunes around, as well as *The Huffington Post*'s list of southern cities not to lose sight of.

Bessemer, however, never finds its way into such spreads. Its court system did make *Time's* pages recently: the atmosphere of a typical day in the courtroom was described as including reconverted church pews for benches, and as embracing such heat and humidity and mildew as to invite brown bugs into the vacant bible holders. So inviting. Those being tried couldn't afford their fines, and so payment plans were being put into effect by private companies.

This, apparently, is one nationwide trend in which Bessemer is more than holding its own.

My hometown boasts neither corporate banks nor thriving mega-businesses like GE, BMW, or Michelin, as Greenville does. So the various "Pawn/Loan" signs that scrape the "Bessemer Super Highway," formerly the main US route from Birmingham to New Orleans, presumably mean something other than vitality.

Something having nothing to do with wealth or hope.

Perhaps the best one can say about these usury shops is that they welcome white and black citizen alike. Their only requirement is that the patron be desperate enough to want to hand over the title of a still-being-paid-for vehicle or the deed to some family heirloom. Then he or she will get back enough money to pay the rent or the light bill or the "Rent-A-Center" bill for that plasma TV.

My mother recently informed me that Bessemer has also been named one of America's top ten most crime-ridden cities. Indeed, crack houses and gunshot echoes refuse to hide from the afternoon light. In fact, the only entity that seems drawn to Bessemer these days is the annual raging tornado that wrecks what's left of Bessemer's formerly stately homes. I've long lamented and occasionally written about Bessemer's decline from a thriving, steel-making, iron-ore laden area—one which included strong ethnic communities including Jewish, Italian, Greek, and Lebanese citizens—to a decaying downtown outline of its former self. The debris of its former glory can't be fully wiped away or even cleaned, in part because the city's sanitation pickup system is so often bankrupt.

Downtown Bessemer used to boast department stores like Pizitz, Sokol's, and Loveman's, and five and dime stores like Woolworth's, McClellan's, Kress, and VJ Elmore. There was an independent record store, The Music Box. Fine clothing shops like I. Rosen, Picards, Kartus Korner also dotted Second Avenue. And manufacturing companies like Zeigler Meats and Long-Lewis Industries employed hundreds. For fine dining experiences there were The Bright Star (which still remains), Romeo's, Edward's Chicken, and the Nix Drive-In (Ok, I'm kidding about that last one).

All of the clean, and much of the dirty money, however, fled Bessemer's limits once the courts reaffirmed in 1964 that the city had to immediately integrate its schools and other public arenas.

Sadly, it has been easy and convenient for me to blame Bessemer's decline on the flight of wealthy white citizens to whiter suburban climes. Easy, because this affluent white exodus left families like mine stuck with other families whose children taught me words like "bastard" and "nooky" in the fourth grade. We were left to watch our only public pool be cemented-over so as to keep "us" from having to share free chlorinated water with "them." We were treated to the draining of Bessemer's West Lake back in the early 70's, so that a natural site of swimming and fishing could be transformed into an enclosed structure where we could walk the cemented floors of Sears, Grant's, Singer's, or hang out in the empty spaces with others of our up-to-no-good tribe. Then, we could eat at Jonathan's, a restaurant that opened that first day the mall did, closed "temporarily for alterations" two weeks later, and never reopened again, though its sign remained fixed in the mall for the next two years.

A symptomatic whimper of Bessemer itself.

I basically left my home city in 1979 when I set off for graduate school. During visits home, I'd note with both alarm and some relief—relief that I had escaped—its lapse into abject poverty. Yet, I never considered, or if I did, never took seriously the real reason for its collapse though I had all the information before me. For I had heard all the stories and had met all the main participants.

Still, you see what you want to see; remember what you choose to. But some things you just can't displace or deny.

You see, until recently, I hadn't believed in Bessemer's curse—the curse of one woman: a woman who lived next door to my family until the winter of 1961.

A woman who tried to burn our house down on a freezing and windy January night.

From the time I was three years old, I noticed this woman. Was scared of this woman and knew she was up to something. I didn't know why I had this feeling, but it was as strong as the feelings of love I felt for my family. Maybe my fear of her stemmed from the fact that her kitchen faced directly across from my bedroom window, and as I glimpsed out that window at night when I was supposed to be sleeping, I saw the furtive shadows behind the kitchen blinds.

Sinister shadows.

Evil shadows.

I feared for all of us, but it was a fear I couldn't name or tell anyone, like the fear most kids have about what lies waiting for us under our beds. The difference was that this fear was a neighbor, yet wasn't I supposed to love our neighbors as ourselves?

Some people come and go from your life; others stay in it whether you want them to or not. Who knows why we remember those we remember, forget those we forget? But with our neighbor Elizabeth Hale? The whole city of Bessemer should remember her, though on most days I believe I'm the only one who does. The only one who knows what happened. The only one who understands the curse she placed on us all, not on the night of the fire, mind you, but a few years later when she died.

And wasn't buried.

"JO ANN, JO ANN! THE HOUSE IS ON FIRE!"

My Nanny's shouts wake me up. I'm four years old and don't

know what to do. The flames haven't reached into my bedroom yet, but they have broken the wall of Nanny's room. In the darkness and confusion, Daddy picks me up; Momma throws my heavy car coat over me and fits my best Sunday shoes—two-toned, black base with white tops—on my feet. But she makes a mistake. My shoes are on the wrong foot, and that scares me.

Even after all this time I admire her for wanting me to survive in my Sunday shoes. I'm remembering Flannery O'Connor's "A Good Man Is Hard to Find," that tale of a grandmother who always dresses to the hilt so that if she is out and has an accident, everyone who sees her will know that she's a lady. For my mother, though, it was a simple case of economics: those shoes cost my father seven dollars retail, and no shoe worth that much would die in a fire if she could help it.

Aided by Nanny, Momma grabs my baby brother Mike, and somehow we all escape into the freezing night. Our neighbors across the street, Margaret and Joe Terry, rush across to help us, to bring us into their house and warm us from that fire.

My Momma nestles me on the Terry's living room couch near the piano where Margaret gives her private lessons to the kids in the neighborhood each weekday afternoon. The Terry kids, especially little Joe and Mary Jane who were closest to my age, look in at me as I lie there. None of us knows exactly what has happened, or what it will mean. Somehow I fall asleep, and the next morning, I walk into their front yard and look down the hill onto our house. Little Joe joins me and puts his arm around my shoulder.

"When I woke up last night and came outside, I could feel that fire on my face," Joe says. "I asked Dad why I could, but all he said was 'Because that fire is really hot!'"

I can't find anything to say to that. I'm just glad that our house didn't burn all the way, though it is badly damaged on that one side: the side that faces the Hale house which is now a heap of smoldering ashes with a blackened chimney next to where the kitchen used to be.

Joe and I stand there looking at the firemen and the police

combing the grounds of what used to be. I see my black, gray, and white cat, Tom, picking his way through the mess. I'd forgotten him and feel bad about it, but he's fine, no worse for the fire.

For the next month we live at the Holiday Inn just outside of town on the Bessemer Super Highway. In those days, the neon Holiday Inn sign, green with glittering lights parading up a right dog-legged angle and leading to a bright star, was so iconic that to see it meant instant joy, almost like seeing the whirling neon of the Ferris Wheel and Roller Coaster at Kiddie-Land, just a few miles up the highway.

Now the sign simply means home.

And during the month that it is our home, we mainly stay in rooms 101 and 102 and take our meals in Michael's restaurant adjoining the inn or at the Super Sandwich Shop in nearby Midfield. For a week, we move into room #1, which has a kitchenette, but then Mike and I come down with the stomach virus, and Momma can't cook at all, so we move back to 101 and 102.

If you ask my mother about this month in her life, she'll shake her head and say: "Lord have mercy, I don't know how we survived. You boys were so sick, and we were all stuck in those little rooms!"

But we did survive. Displaced, but not defeated. We had a good insurance agent, Joe Terry, and a community of friends, though not necessarily neighbors, who helped us regain our neighborhood footing.

When the month was over, we moved back into our restored house, where only occasionally the residue of the fire announced itself through certain smells or the living vision of my mother's scorched wedding dress that she nevertheless continued to keep in the upper cabinet of the hallway just outside Nanny's room. Though it was ruined, I was glad she kept it, my Momma's wedding dress.

I think it took me that entire month of displacement to realize that fires don't just happen. I was never allowed to play with my Momma's Ronson lighter or touch the stove at all. I didn't know of electrical fires or of over-stocking outlets. For that month, what I knew was that our house partially burned and the Hale's was destroyed. We were lucky and they weren't. That's what I thought anyway. I didn't consider the truth of my fears, maybe because I was too little to put it together. Or maybe I was just glad we weren't hurt and relieved to know that our house would be ours again.

But soon I heard the fuller story of what happened that night with the family who lived next door. The family whose house burned to the ground. The family we never saw again.

My Momma still has a picture of the Hale house in an old family album. It's in the background, looming over Mary Jane Terry and me: two childhood playmates who don't recognize this danger. The house had one story, a pitched roof, and black siding. The siding is actually black tarpaper, an unfinished house-to-be.

It seems like four or five people lived in the Hale house, but now, the only two I remember clearly are Elizabeth, and her husband, WD. He was called WD though we kids heard it as "DubbyDee." DubbyDee drove an old blue delivery van, which was somewhat fitting, because he did deliver things.

Houses, actually. He moved houses: jacked them up, slid them onto flatbed trailers, and hauled them to places where the houses, if not the families inside them, were wanted.

In my mind I see him looking like "The Skipper" from "Gilligan's Island," and I think DubbyDee did wear a sea captain's hat. He wore overalls too, Momma said, and he was big and round and seemed pretty jolly. I yelled "Hey DubbyDee" at him every time I saw him pull up in that van, and he seemed to enjoy the name and the attention. I remember my Momma talking to him, too, and I didn't see any difference in her friendliness to him from what she showed to any other neighbor. For DubbyDee, too, was a fixture in my world—a world I thought, as most kids do, would never change or have anything come or go from it.

Elizabeth Hale wasn't a fixture, though, as much as a fleeting presence. In my mind, she resembled "Mrs. Larch" from "The Andy Griffith Show," that lady who asks Andy to call her cousin in Colorado while he's vacationing in Hollywood, because, after all, "he'll be so close." Elizabeth Hale and Mrs. Larch wore their dark hair in a bun on the back, a severe and unbecoming look for any housewife.

But then Elizabeth Hale wasn't "any housewife," and so I came to associate her with a much more frightening figure.

I could never watch all of *The Wizard of Oz* when it came on TV each April. I couldn't make it past that part when Dorothy looks out her bedroom window and sees the evil Miss Gulch transform into the still eviler Wicked Witch of the West.

That window thing forever linked the Wicked Witch with Elizabeth Hale for me.

I'd never look long at Elizabeth Hale's kitchen window. I'd part my curtains as slightly as I could for fear of being seen by my witch—of having her look right in my eyes, just as happens to Dorothy when the Wicked Witch turns and cackles right at her. Dorothy isn't sure who this is. What has happened to Miss Gulch? What is happening as her house flies through the Kansas whirlwind evening?

Of course, what was happening through my window was probably nothing more than the Hales cleaning up after supper. I wondered why were there so many people there? Momma said that DubbyDee's stepmother lived there too, and that they always had visitors coming to stay with them, sometimes for weeks:

"I didn't know what they did there, but it was something. Once, your Daddy said he could see in their side window, and they were having some kind of séance. At least that's what he thought they were doing."

Calling up what spirits. For what evil purpose?

Of course I'd fall asleep soon after my nightly watch, but I always felt that if at any time of the night I peeled my curtain back again, those shadows would be there waiting for me. And if they caught me looking, they would get me and take me away to some place, and I'd never see my family again.

It turned out that I wasn't so wrong in my fears. It turned out that I might have been more perceptive than any of us could have figured.

❀

"Yes ma'am," I heard Momma saying on the phone not long after we moved back into our house. "They burned their own house down! They didn't care which way the wind was blowing or that ours or anybody else's house might catch fire too."

The story goes that they sat in DubbyDee's van in the alley and watched it burn. Whether they ate or drank as they watched, or did some kind of dance as the Shaw children claimed, I can't say.

I don't know if anyone ever could or did prove arson, but I never saw either of them again, though once, Momma did:

"I ran into that old WD Hale at the grocery store today. Said they were all living in a trailer now, but he didn't say where. He laughed like we were old friends, but he never said anything about that house, or our house either."

And that was it for several years until we heard what we thought was the last Hale story, the one where the witch finally died.

After over fifty years, it's confusing to get all the dates right—the timing of when something was said and what it meant to me then. For instance, at some point when I was four or five I'm sure Momma told me that Elizabeth Hale herself declared that she was a witch. That she could tell the future and cast spells. But maybe this never happened; maybe it was just my impression of a next-door-neighbor who was creepy and forbidding, whose comings and goings were shadowy and threatening. My Momma at this time was only thirty years old, and it might be that when

I saw or thought of her next to the Witch, I got really scared. For compared to this older, threatening woman, my Momma seemed so small, so weak, and today I'd say so impotent.

Scared as I was of all that could happen then, I clearly remember one afternoon sitting in the rain beneath the enormous hydrangea bush on the side of the house and crying as the water beat down beside me. Crying because the Hales were there and no one understood who they really were and what they might do to us. I couldn't tell anyone why I was crying; I just didn't have those words.

I wonder now if my Momma ever cried. Or whether, if I had told her why I was crying, she'd have understood me. If she could have comforted my fears. And her own.

And despite all that seemed to be normal, despite that DubbyDee was so friendly when I saw him regardless of whatever his wife was or did, I understood that I should never walk in their yard. Should never ring their bell for Halloween. I knew our family would never exchange Christmas presents, food ingredients, or any other form of normal neighborliness with them. And even had I been just a bit older, I would never have sneaked up to a window in their house and peered in, as I did with the Bruce house on the other side of the Hales.

Even as a little kid, I would sneak looks into the Bruce's side windows, hoping to find the treasure I knew they had hidden somewhere. With their fine piano in the front window, Mrs. Bruce's pearls and fancy wide-brimmed hats, surely they had treasure stashed in a safe somewhere in that house. But despite my sneaking around, all I ever saw was Old Man Bruce's face. You'd think the prospect of his face and his hand banging on the window telling me to go home would have frightened me and kept me away. But it didn't. He wasn't even that scary, even though behind his own coke-bottle glasses, I could see that his eyes were clearly crossed. After all, he was just a grumpy old man.

In any case, neither he nor his house scared me like the Hale house did, that house from which I could never hide.

So losing the Hale house, never seeing the Hale family again, was a relief I thought would last forever.

But just a couple of years after the fire, over a supper of Momma's famous Country Captain chicken and rice on an early fall evening, the Hales returned in a final burning vapor, as Momma announced to us all that the wicked witch was dead.

Is it still funny today that in southern homes, the most shocking and lurid subjects find their way to our ears during a pleasant meal?

Was it this supper moment when I first knew that Bessemer was in trouble? Though clearly social, political, and even religious forces had been at work for many years to send Bessemer on its downward spiral, I think the words I heard over this supper changed me and my hometown forever.

"I ran into Isobel Millsap today at Curry's, and you'll never guess what! [And Momma never gives any of us time to guess anyway but just keeps going] Elizabeth Hale died last week!"

None of us even had the time to register fully that this was "the" Elizabeth Hale. Nanny had her coffee cup poised mid-level between table and lips, and Daddy was still mopping up the chicken gravy with his angel biscuit. Mike was in his high chair, and I just stared at Momma feeling a sort of relief I never knew I could feel.

"But here's the strange part," Momma hurried on. "Isobel said that that woman wanted her body to be cremated and her ashes taken up in a plane and then scattered all over Bessemer! And today, they did it."

"My Lord," Nanny said. "What do you mean, Jo Ann? Her ashes? You mean they're out there?"

"And we can walk on 'em," I cried.

"That's exactly what I mean. They're everywhere. Can you believe she did that? I always said that woman was hateful, and now she's had her last laugh on Bessemer. As if Bessemer or anybody else ever did anything to her! It's like she was trying to get back at the whole town!"

I'm sure there was further talk then on whatever revenge Elizabeth Hale thought she had to take, of the fires and spells she cast. There might have even been talk of the still that the Hales supposedly ran in their basement. I don't really remember, though, because I had never heard of anyone being cremated. For that matter, I had never even been to a funeral or seen a dead body.

So while I considered burning a body to ashes, I also had to consider tossing those ashes from the skies of Bessemer on a bright October afternoon. I had to consider walking on those ashes, breathing them in. Did they find me at school that day? Did they make it through the oak trees and pecans? Were they resting in my dog's house underneath our back steps?

I had a glimpse then into a world I never knew I'd have to reckon with. It was too much to take in and not enough to understand. In any case, that was the story, and to my knowledge even now, it's true.

Ashes themselves eventually disintegrate, becoming one with the ground and atmosphere. We no longer see them, and even before we forget that we can't see them, they have vanished from our minds.

But not completely from our memory, as anyone still living in my family will tell you. Like my Momma, today:

"I'm glad they left. After the fire, they wanted to bring a trailer back up to that property and live next to us again, but we wouldn't let that happen. Honest to God, I think Elizabeth Hale would as soon as killed you as look at you. I know I was scared of her. They say she used to ride bareback horses in the carnival, but I don't know where she came from. She said she was part Indian, but I don't believe it. But she was something else, I'll tell you!"

I was laughing at this now, in that way we have of laughing at carnival things—spook houses and two-headed calves—that might have once, but can no longer get at us.

"But ol' DubbyDee wasn't so bad was he?"

"Bad? For as long as they lived there he was bad, and they lived there for decades. He and his daddy made Hale's Quick

Relief, an elixir they claimed was good for animals and humans. Yeah, HQR, they called it! And WD could cook good barbecue. He made a pit out of an old store cooler. But he was mean. I remember my mother got so upset at his brother, because after my brother died, my mother gave WD's brother all my brother's clothes, and he never said thank you, or I appreciate it, kiss my foot, or anything. That hurt my mother bad."

"I guess it did."

"But that WD! After they moved away, I heard another thing, though I don't remember who told me. But whoever it was said they saw WD running down the Super Highway, you know, where Bob Sykes is now, and he was chasing after some dog. He was trying to..."

This was one of the pauses I feared, because I thought Momma couldn't find the words she wanted to say. That had been happening after her most recent operation, a residue of all that sedative. But it wasn't that she couldn't find the words then; it was just that she couldn't say those words to me, or possibly to anybody.

"Chasing a dog...what do you mean Momma?...Oh. You don't mean...he was trying to...?"

"That's what they said anyway. Someone stopped him, though, thank the Lord. They call that bestiality."

Yes, they do.

"I was sure glad after they were gone!"

Gone. But is anyone ever really gone? What with those ashes and all.

As I sift through the remains of those years, and though I might be the only one who sees it this way—and one of the only ones who still remembers—I realize that Elizabeth Hale accomplished what she intended. She became a part of Bessemer's lore and its continuing present for as long as it lasts. She placed her hex on the town, and it was never the same after. You may say that the city's descent came about because of its inability and refusal to deal with integration. And you may be right.

Still, there are other forces in the air. Forces emanating from certain moods or powers that cause conditions to change. Cause feelings to stir and never settle down. Cause us to mistrust our community and the good neighbors in it. For if we breathe in too much steel industry smog, if we are exposed for too many months and years to mosquito-spraying trucks, or burned asbestos walls, or incinerated plastic, or brown bugs in our bibles, what does it do to our thinking? Our way of life?

What did it do to us all when we took our breaths during those uncertain hours on a sunny, cool, October day?

Do we even know, and can we even say?

When a neighbor sets fire to your house, even indirectly, can you ever fully account for the damage? Can you ever live in peace again, even if the fear has moved away? Can you ever know, even with all the years in between, what has and has not been scorched?

Can you satisfactorily conclude, good neighbor, that all those Cash-for Gold or EZ Loan palaces aren't the dying embers of a fire that no one saw coming, and that no one ever fully put out: A fire that some of us watched, others of us fled, and none of us much remembers any more, even when we do stop to think of all that we had and lost?

5
Church-Ladies

No one cares more about church attendance, proper church decorum, and the inner workings of the church body than do its grandmothers. Think of that "Andy Griffith" episode where the Mayberry church has been bequeathed a sum of several hundred dollars. The church fathers vote to use those funds to strengthen the building's foundation, one side of which has sunk by six inches; the female elders, the church grandmothers, vote for new choir robes, the old ones having become tattered and faded. One grizzled little fellow named Elmo votes for a pool table for the men's social hall, but there's always an Elmo opting for pool or bingo or shuffleboard. Though Logic lies with the men, Emotion, Determination, and, it seems, Divine Will lie with the grandmothers. Aunt Bee and cohort Clara Edwards won't even speak to, much less cook for the men during the debate, particularly to ringleader and County Clerk, Howard Sprague. A compromise, of course, finally carries the day—involving a flood, though not of Biblical proportions—and thus in the end, all are pleased and once again poor beleaguered Andy and Opie get to partake in Aunt Bee's ritually-famous fried chicken and apple pie a la mode supper. But had the compromise not been brokered, don't you know who would have won in the end, even if that meant founding their own church just to get even?

I know that "saving souls" and "preaching the gospel" are usually associated with fiery male ministers. In my offering, though, it's the grandmothers who have remained steadfast. Since they take salvation as a given for all those gracing the church's inner body, other notions preoccupy their church minds and hearts: Rules, respect, and social standing in the eyes of their beloved community. These and the reality that for them, their church is also their "home."

In my youth, grandmothers could not be official stewards of the church. Yet, as I view these long-ago days, I realize that my primary religious instruction came not from Dr. Sansberry or Brother Frederick who raised the sanctuary roof with their sermons, nor from my friends' daddies, the ivory-suited ushers and offertory collectors who, after performing their duties, often collected *themselves* in the church office to count the money, sip more coffee, and discuss the previous day's football game. No, I learned all I did about the church and its culture from the grandmothers who never tried to "save our souls" so much as to build character into them, through often unplanned lessons of decorum, devotion, and love.

Because my own maternal grandmother, "Nanny," established herself as an institution unto herself within Bessemer's First Methodist Church-bosom, I could never hope to escape the adoration and admonishment of the other Church ladies who were Nanny's best friends and card-playing cronies. Conferring upon her contemporaries the right to give me any direction they wanted, Nanny's blessings on her church sisters resulted, in Woody Allen's immortal words, in my having to "survive being raised by more than one [grand]mother." And I did survive, though I also committed and suffered through certain offenses.

1. Skipping Steps and Landing on My Butt.

Why is skipping steps so catastrophic to the elderly sensibility? Yes it's true that one may trip going either up or down a set of steps. I learn this truth first-hand at age six when I fall flat on my butt on the deep brown marble-tiled floor of our church basement banquet hall, trying to leap in one bound the set of two steps before me. My failure, of course, doesn't bode well for my future athletic glory.

Naturally, I don't accomplish this feat in the privacy of my own shame; I turn red when I make a mistake of any sort, regardless of who isn't watching. I'm sure I've turned a deep scarlet after spilling my cereal in front of my cat who, naturally, is all-too-happy about my error. On this day of step-skipping, though, at first I think that no one has seen me, my mother lingering out by the car to help my little brother Mike out of his car seat. After my fall, I jump to my feet before Mom can enter and see me. Now, if only the janitor hasn't already swept that day so that no grimy residue soils my clothes.

Well, I'm lucky there at least, but what has slipped my mind is the specially-called Women's Missionary Society meeting, the occasion for which we've arrived to retrieve my Nanny. As I turn to seek my mother's safety, I hear the voice of my primary-level Sunday School teacher, Miss Pridmore, an otherwise sweet, gentle, and kind soul in her early eighties:

"Buddy Barr! You come back here right now and go down those steps in the proper way!"

How, I ask now, do adults always know that a child isn't hurt, but only dazed, confused, and embarrassed after such a fall? How does Miss Pridmore know that I haven't twisted an ankle or broken a wrist? And why can't she discern that I surely didn't want to fall and that the foolishness of my act and the resulting bruises will be lesson enough? Why can't she "intuit" that I won't attempt this maneuver again? However, as if she has caught a typo in a formal business letter or college application, she determines that only one course of action can be taken to remedy my church waywardness: the entire episode must be redone.

"Start at the door and come into this room like you've been taught to, and walk down those steps as if you aren't a young heathen! This is God's house after all!"

And God doesn't like little boys to skip steps, not even in His basement. I'm sure that if I had been reading my Bible carefully, I would have heard the admonishment somewhere in Exodus, Leviticus, or the Book of Judges that "Thou shalt not skip church steps."

So I walk back outside, re-enter the basement door, and calmly, methodically, descend those two steps, one at a time, under Miss Pridmore's approving eye, forgetting now why I had been in such a hurry in the first place.

"Now, isn't that better?"

"Yes Miss Pridmore."

I look around, and though neither my Mom nor Nanny is in sight, I know they're aware of what has happened, for like God in the days of my childhood, their eyes see all.

Miss Pridmore "retired" the next year. In her place, one of the younger church mothers took over, a woman with five kids herself: a woman whose kids were, as my Mother described them, "Holy Terrors." These kids ran through the church halls, soiled their clothes not five minutes after arriving at the church, and of course skipped all kinds of steps in the three-story structure that our Methodist God had built for us in Bessemer. I never believed I'd miss Miss Pridmore, but after seeing them, I learned then that all things were possible in God's house.

2. Talking or Making Otherwise Avoidable and Unintelligible Sounds During the Service.

Miss Ruthie Hamner, one of Nanny's bridge-playing cronies, seems to have rented a room in our house, since no card party can be held without her. She doesn't drive, and so she depends on her best friend, Miss Ora Latham, to chauffeur her around. Somehow, even when Miss Ora is out-of-commission, Miss Ruthie finds her way to a seat at Nanny's fold-out bridge table. Fortunately, Miss Ora rarely misses a date and plays bridge expertly, so she and Miss Ruthie make a suitable pair. Miss Ora's hair is whiter than Ivory soap, a sheen complemented by the ruby red lipstick she consistently wears which, given her constant smile, warms me to her, more so than most of the other grandmotherly card-players. Still, she kind of scares me too, because each time she enters our house, she insists that I tell her the name of my girlfriend. This question truly terrifies me because it takes for granted that I have a girlfriend, and just how would Miss Ora know that? Also, her smile never changes regardless of my response. And if I say "No one," that smile is accompanied by a most-knowing wink.

Miss Ruthie, by contrast, wears her grizzled skin on a rather horsy face. Her eyes remind me exactly of those on the miniature bust of a Gay Nineties man in straw hat with long, curly sideburns that sits on the front entry table in my other grandmother's apartment. His severely upturned nose and his piercing brown eyes lend him a shocked affect, as if he has just seen another hemline go up, or spied a recently bobbed hairdo. His eyes, always staring at me no matter what part of the room I stand in, are God's eyes. I know this as surely as I know later that my mother only visits this grandmother out of protest.

And since this god-like figure's eyes are Miss Ruthie's eyes, Ruthie Hamner is God.

Miss Ruthie sits on the next-to-back pew in the sanctuary during Sunday service, directly in front of my friends and me who, being average teens, have no particular interest in the service. Each week we cram into that back row so that we can grope each other's knees, pass love notes, play word games and tic-tac-toe, and generally try not to give in totally to disruptive giggles.

The word game I like best—hangman—passes the time most efficiently. The hidden phrase we choose usually spells out the name of one of the various and obscure 60's rock bands that we love, or at least pretend to love in order to impress each other. Once, I used "Spooky Tooth," causing my friend Don to hang himself in seven straight moves and then punch me in the arm as if it were my fault.

Miss Ruthie, though, has taken it on herself to monitor, modify, or put a stop to our inappropriate behavior before it gets cranked up.

Of course, she can't say anything to us because then she'd just be making more noise and calling attention to herself, and someone, the choirmaster perhaps, might believe that she's a co-conspirator *with* us, doing her best to stay alive as Brother Frederick drones on. So here is how she takes us to task when we pass the limit of proper quiet: She turns three-quarters of the way in her seat, her eyes the size of that God-like figurine, and she examines us all, up and down the pew. Her stare lingers on me two or three counts longer than on my friends, as if she needs to remind me that next Wednesday, *Oh Yes*, she'll be seeing me in our living room, cards and chicken salad sandwiches in hand, and then we'll reckon with each other. Upon her stare, I drop the pencil I'm using to save my hanged soul, stash the paper in the book holder on the pew's back, and jam my hands under my legs, feigning my confused and would-be innocence.

All of us grow quiet then and return to our best behavior. For maybe three minutes. But as the clamor stirs anew, she invariably makes another turn, only this time the stare, since it clearly hasn't turned the trick, transforms itself into what Miss Ruthie must consider a more severe non-verbal warning: One that should scare any irreverent child.

She begins blinking.

Like an ocular Morse code, she expresses a complexity of meaning with every blink, saying to one and all of us nestled on that back row:

"You are rude and disrespectful children, and I'd banish you from this service except that doing so would defeat the purpose of Sunday Morning which is to save your everlasting souls, and so while I don't know what the preacher is talking about either, you pretend and I'll pretend, and if you refuse, then all my blinking will be for nothing, and I'll be just another old maid, when you know and I know I'm doing this for your own good because what I really want to be is your grandmother. So there. And Amen."

Or maybe that's just my conscience speaking. After several

moments of such "blink-code," Miss Ruthie turns back to the front. But Don, the baddest of the church bad boys—he has brothers who play in a rock-n-roll band aptly named "Mother Savage"—and not one to let a moment for a good impersonation pass, sits up straight, turns toward us on the left and right, and begins his variation of the "Hamner blink." Of course we crack up all over again, thus causing yet another turn of Miss Ruthie's head. Usually, Don anticipates the timing of her head-turns, but on one momentous Sunday, as he is turning to the front again, Miss Ruthie catches him in mid-blink. For a few seconds, their mutual blinking creates a kind of harmony unrivaled by the tenors and altos in the loft above.

If I say to you now that Miss Ruthie was really sweet and that though I laughed at his antics, I really *wanted* to kick Don's ass but couldn't (not only because he would have beaten me to a pulp but because what teenager ever sided with a grandmother over a peer?), you'd believe me, right?

3. Talking Loudly in the Sanctuary Even Though No One Else Is There.

Some call her "The Gargoyle," and in truth, she does watch over our church benevolently, as in true gargoyle lore. Her actual name: Mary Morey Moore; she has two daughters, the younger of whom is named after her. I wonder if that means that "Little Mary Morey" is a "junior." "No," my parents inform me, "girls can't be juniors."

"What can they be then?" But as usual, I am dismissed with a wave and a "Leave me alone now, I'm busy."

I never knew that mothers might name their daughters after themselves. If I had been a girl, would my mother have considered naming me after herself: "Little Jo Ann?" What might this do to a fragile psyche?

For Mary Morey "junior," her psyche claims within her a need to be right all the time. Three years my senior, she comes over regularly to play with my brother and me, "with the boys," as she puts it. We play "Hillbilly" sometimes, and she's our "Ma," who rules with an iron hand. She controls my brother's air rifle, the seat in the corner where bad boys go to be punished, and she decides just when the game should end, usually by aiming the air rifle at one of us and disintegrating the family. Pointing that rifle, though, no matter how harmless we consider it, provokes my Nanny into the most primitive state of rage that I've ever seen.

"Don't' you ever, EVER, aim any gun at anyone."

Nanny would be close to tears at this point, and I don't know if we're laughing at the picture she makes—old, gray-haired, stooped woman descending upon our "Ma,"—or out of our own fear that she knows best and is trying to protect us against our own worst instincts. From age three I've owned "play-guns." Though my parents never buy me real "caps," I can make every gun noise known to man as I massacre Cowboys or Indians, ride into World War II army battles, or even, on rare occasions, rob an Old West bank. So while I can play with guns and make gun sounds, I just can't aim those guns within my Nanny's sight. I wonder if someone aimed a gun at a person she loved once. And does this explain why she reminds us every other week NOT to allow certain of her own relatives, like the apocryphal drunkard Arn (aka Iron or Ourn) Terry, to ever enter our house?

But Mary Morey, Sr. enters our house frequently and whenever she appears at our front door, it's her teeth that you see first; teeth that have earned her the moniker "The Gargoyle."

Accompanying those teeth, her voice rivals any minister's for pitch, timbre, and volume. When we drive up to the church's 19th St. entrance—the closest to the office where "The Gargoyle" stations herself as church secretary—even if our windows are raised in wintertime, we hear her voice rolling out from her office door:

"Yay baby, that's what I told her. No, No, 'MayMoray' says don't go to that store, they'll steal ALL yo money."

She speaks so rapidly that five words become one, and her own name comes out as not only one word, but one *syllable*.

Though she's a friend to all who walk into the church, she's also a gargoyle—a true force of nature—and someone I don't want to reckon with in any other way but good.

And yet I do; I tempt Gargoyle fate. While my mother and Nanny are visiting the church one morning, Mike and I are playing hide-and-seek on the church's main floor. I hide in the sanctuary, behind a pew on the eighth or ninth row. I hear him enter this hallowed ground, stepping nearer and nearer to my improvised manger. The red-velvet carpet and pew cushions enable me to spring high at just the right moment. I scare the devil out of him, and my shout, his scream, and our combined laughter echo around the sanctuary's stained glass and cathedral ceiling. Echoes and echoes, layers upon layers of semi-barbarian roars until the Gargoyle descends, or actually, sticks her head through the very door that the preacher strides through on Sundays to ascend to his anointed pulpit, and blasts away:

"Buddy and Mikey Barr! What is the meaning of this? Who do you think you are? Don't you know this is God's special place? I'm gonna wear both of you out, and your mama won't mind if I do! I'm ashamed of you both. I know you know better!"

Her face is a mask of outrage, contempt, and rebuke. Her teeth glare as fiercely as her eyes. If I have never before contemplated the wrath of the angry God who in whichever chapter of whichever book leveled the cities of Sodom and Gomorrah, turned Lot's wife into a pillar of salt, and thereby reduced the poor guy to a homeless widower, I do now.

She keeps her word and tells my Momma and my Nanny, and they continue the "lecture of shame" for the entire ride home. My brother and I promise never to play in God's house again, and we keep that promise for a few weeks.

While Mary Morey never forgets our transgression, she does soften toward us eventually. Maybe in part because she and "Little Mary Morey" are frequent guests at our house. They don't live in our neighborhood—one of the oldest and formerly finest in the town, whose southside hills allow us to gaze over the sleeping city. No, they live across town, but definitely not the exclusive enclave of Lakewood. Their exact address was #4 Third Avenue, a block from Center Street, in a row of houses that you might term double-wide shotgun shacks. Though they eat many lunches and dinners with us, the Mary Moreys politely turn down more invitations than they ever issue in reciprocation. In fact, I never set foot in their house. And if one day, at my request, Mom hadn't driven me past their place, I might have believed that the church actually is their home, for aren't they always there?

In the end, I'm glad they're always at the church, because it comforts me to think of them there, keeping this second home from ever being empty. I don't know how the Gargoyle spends her waking hours as secretary. What exactly does a church secretary do? But then, maybe that lighted building is a sanctuary, a true haven for a woman whose home will grow increasingly dark when her daughter and namesake finally leaves her.

For Little Mary Morey eventually marries a boy named Bruce, her married name becoming Mary Morey Moore Murchison. And one day they'll have a little girl, too, but I'll never know that child's name.

I do remember her wedding, though. For the first time ever, I see Little Mary Morey cry. My hillbilly "Ma" absolutely bawls as she proceeds out of the sanctuary on the arm of her new husband. Is she relieved to be married...or something else? For some reason, her tears don't seem joyous.

I remember too that Big Mary Morey's foot is broken, and as she walks the aisle in God's special place, the last person to be seated before her daughter marches in, she strides with a dignified hobble, her leg-cast accessorizing her floor-length, sea-green gown. Her eyes, though, are cast heavenward, not exactly as if she's thanking or praising God, but more like she's seeking the credit that she believes is surely her due. When she exits the church, she walks right by me, but since she is gazing upward, our eyes never meet. And hers never flicker, not even once. Just like those of a church gargoyle.

4. Playing Bible Games With Warts

In all of my Sunday school, Bible school, and wasting-time-while-my-mother-and-Nanny-toiled-at-Church-days, one figure stands out amongst the other "grandmothers" there: Miss Pauline Jones.

Miss Pauline, short and stooped, never seems to age, proving that it is possible for some people to be born whole at the age of seventy-two. Moving quickly, assertively, she always seems to know where she's heading. She wears a silver, flexible watchband with a half-dollar-sized dial turned to the inner part of her right forearm; I've only seen men wear watches like this. The full-length shifts she wears even to Sunday morning service make her seem as if she is engulfed in a canvas tent; these shifts have no discernible shape and are neutrally-colored in tints of cadmium, off-white, quicksilver, and palest blue. And then, her shoes. I know nothing of orthopedic shoes. Did Miss Pauline wander into Bessemer Memorial Hospital and take a cast-off pair of nurse's brogans? By contrast, my Nanny wears open-toed, black old ladies' pumps—sturdy *and* high-heeled. She prefers "French Nouvelle Vague," while Miss Pauline chooses "Soviet Realism."

Miss Pauline's iron-gray hair is styled in a modified page-boy, a bit shorter than that of Sunday comics' Prince Valiant. Her silver-toned, metal-framed, rectangular glasses might be the envy of Mods everywhere, but for her, they only magnify her milky-blue eyes giving her an overall bearing of friendliness and good will, albeit with a touch of what? Recklessness? Homelessness? She has to have good will because, apparently, she lives at the church too, perhaps in one of the twelve basement rooms used for Bible school classes every summer. Actually it just seems that she lives in God's house, because one day, as we're driving down Arlington Avenue, away from church, I see her walking, fast-paced and head down.

"There's Miss Pauline! Where on earth is she going?"

"Right over there," Mom gestures.

"You mean she lives there?"

It was a smallish gray A-framed house, right next to the railroad tracks: A house I've seen many times, and one that I've never failed to despair of because it's so little, so worn-down, and so very near the trains that blare their presence throughout the night, making it impossible, I think, for anyone in such close proximity to sleep long or soundly.

"Why are you so concerned with where Miss Pauline lives?"

"I don't know, just wonderin'."

When a kid says "I don't know," he assuredly does even if he refuses or is unable to explain himself. I wonder where Miss Pauline lives just as I wonder about certain stray dogs who pass our house and whom my parents always declare have some home, "some*where*." Usually, I trust their wisdom and forget the dog in question. Miss Pauline, my recurring worry, poses a different dilemma, however; regarding her, I can't be sure what, or whom, to trust.

Still, it feels good to know that she has a house like everyone else does, even if I wouldn't have wanted to live there: A house like "normal" people have, even if, deep-down, I get the feeling that the word "normal" doesn't exactly apply to Miss Pauline.

For outside of that one time, I never see Miss Pauline away from the church. She doesn't frequent the beauty parlor that the other church grandmothers frequent, and by beauty parlor I mean the side-door entrance to the home of someone named Flora or Alberta. Miss Pauline neither plays bridge nor tries her hand at any other card game that I know of. At least, she is never invited to any at our house. Nor do I ever see her eating lunch at the various sandwich shops in downtown Bessemer, just a six-block walk from her home. Come to think of it, I've never seen her eating at all, except during the week of our Vacation Bible School.

No matter the weather or other external exigencies, Miss Pauline attends both Sunday morning and evening services without fail, usually sitting in the front pew, not necessarily next to anyone in particular. Often, however, another parishioner stations herself close enough to Miss Pauline to reassure a small boy that at least Miss Pauline has *some* friends. After I join the choir at age fourteen, from my perch above and behind the altar, I watch Miss Pauline during the services. She stares rapturously, or at least raptly, at the preacher, though none of our Methodist preachers is exactly the "rapt" type.

During the offering Miss Pauline never fails to put in her dollar—I can see the George Washington so clearly that it seems like it's the same Federal Reserve Note each week. One evening, as the plate passes her and travels on down the row, I observe a pillar of our congregation handing the plate on without putting one penny in. Outraged, and on the verge of tears, I report the offense later to my mother, asking how, if Miss Pauline can manage to put a dollar in the plate each week, Mr. Samuels can just sit there stony-faced and miserly. But Momma isn't having any of my righteous indignation:

"Verne Samuels tithes his money! Don't you dare believe he doesn't give to that church! He's a faithful steward, and speaking of giving, how much of your allowance do you put in?"

So why *was* I being so defensive about this funny little woman? Though I vow to start adding my quarter the next week, I still know what I know, feel what I feel about Miss Pauline: That we share a history—an episode that will never mean anything to anybody *but* me. A time one summer during Bible school when I am five years old.

During that August week of supposed fun, crafts, and games (and pledging allegiance to the Christian Flag), one rosy morning twenty or thirty kids stand outside on the church grounds playing Red Rover. The rules of Red Rover—in fact the actual ability to participate in Red Rover—depend solely on each side's holding hands as tightly as possible so as to prevent any of the opposing side's players from breaking through your ranks when they are "called" to "come over."

A game requiring so little physical prowess shouldn't pose a problem, even for awkward boys like me. Except that in the one necessary body part to play Red Rover, I have a problem, or rather, a multitude of them. Warts. Not one or two random and strategically hidden warts, but whole groupings on the top of my hand. Plainly visible groupings that appear as mounds not unlike a pattern of fire-ant hills in the cracks of a summer sidewalk. Twenty-two warts on my right hand alone, and on my left, just one, though it is twice the size as the largest one on my right and covers completely the second knuckle of my ring finger.

As part of our special Bible school Red Rover rules—and no doubt to encourage some form of future investment in the church—boys and girls have to alternate standing next to each other in their respective Red Rover lines. To my knowledge, no guy has ever recoiled in horror at my warts; since most believe you get them from handling or being peed on by frogs, it's actually a badge of honor for boys to have one (and I mean ONE!). But girls: Touching frogs, toads, reptiles of any sort? Or touching any boy touched by them?

To be honest and fair, and righteous, I know to my very soul that I would have refused to take the hand of any "Wart-Boy" like me. So I really can't blame the girl standing next to me on my right—an "older woman" of perhaps ten, Jody Self—who, when she looks down at the hand she's about to clasp, starts yelling "OOOOOhhhhh, YUCK, YUCK!!! I'm not touching YOUR hand!" And then she actually and very actively runs to the opposing side and grabs for dear life the hand of Donny Thomas, a very cool guy. Years later my mother will hear him say "Fuck You!" to another kid in the high school parking lot.

It's not like being wart-rejected has never happened before. But you never get used to it, or at least I never do. Two years later, after Compund-40 treatments and skin-doctors' attempts to slice off wart-layers on a weekly basis—leaving my hand bloody and in a virtual cast for several days afterwards—modern technology steps in, in the form of an electric needle that will "burn off" those warts, leaving me, of course, with a wart-free but perpetually scarred right hand.

But that's still to come. Now, when Jody flees, I am left without a Red Rover partner on my right, and no one exactly rushes in to fill the void. No one, that is, except Miss Pauline:

"I'll hold your hand Buddy."

Until that moment I didn't even know that she knew my name. She takes my hand, holds it firmly, and for the rest of that Bible school week, whenever a game commences, she's at my side, holding my hand if I want her to.

Which, of course, I always do.

I know *now* that she was crazy, that the adults tolerated her presence, and I know now that they wouldn't have trusted her, as they would have the other grandmothers, with the duties of actual babysitting.

I hear my Mother's voice so clearly, somewhere between these Bible School days and this present moment:

"She was crazy as a loon! Everyone knew about Miss Pauline. We never believed she'd hurt anyone, and we did feel sorry for her, but I wouldn't have left her alone with you or your brother."

So who exactly was this woman, my Red Rover friend, my grandmother-in-waiting? All I know is that Mr. Samuels never held my hand, and that for my benefit, Miss Pauline always *was* there, especially when no one else could or would be.

But as I grow out of such childhood needs and become a teenager, I quit acknowledging Miss Pauline, in front of my friends anyway. I move on through high school, and when I leave for college, Miss Pauline becomes just another old woman whose life ceases to register on me. So I know neither the time, place, nor occasion of her passing, or whether she was alone or in a hospital or hospice. Nor do I know where she is buried, who paid for and made the arrangements, or whether anyone remembers her at all now, much less visits the local cemetery where she may or may not reside. I thought I had forgotten Miss Pauline but have recently discovered that she enjoys being visited—that all she ever wanted was for someone, a grandson say, to hold her hand.

5. I Leave My Nanny.

I'm convinced that my Nanny owns the church. I don't mean that I think she has any papers, deeds, or makes a profit on its use, but since she can be found there more regularly than anywhere else, commanding everyone inside to do her bidding, I consider the entire church domain to be hers. Which makes the fact that she never attends any service but Easter all-the-more mysterious and unsettling.

I see her in the church kitchen, a basement suite of rooms that Julia Child or Betty Crocker would have killed to own. She coordinates Ladies' luncheons, family night suppers, and on Sunday evenings—when my Mom and Dad, my brother and I are fifteen miles away at our weekly visit to my other grandmother's—Nanny prepares the meal for the Methodist Youth Fellowship: Chili, hot dogs, burgers, or spaghetti. She reports to me later that night who all attended; how many burgers Karen Pearson ate; who was forced to give Ross McIntyre a ride home. As I hear her tales and think of her, bottled Coke in hand, in the midst of kids I long to be near, she seems to me to be everyone else's grandmother and not mine, and the thought of sharing her with everyone unsettles me.

I don't know how much or even *if* she receives payment for her services. I don't know if, after the supper, she attends the evening service—a service that usually attracts no more then forty or fifty congregants (as opposed to the 300+ who attend morning service). I don't know if the gathered kids of MYF appreciate what she does for them, love her for it, or think of her as their grandmother too. She has no official title other than "Kitchen: Mrs. G.C. Terry," a line in our weekly church bulletin. Everyone in her circle, in my parents' and in mine, refers to her as Miz Terry, never Miz GC, and certainly never Ellen, her given name.

Though Nanny doesn't attend Sunday morning service, on those Sabbath mornings of my childhood, she nevertheless rises first, retrieving the morning paper and preparing herself a light breakfast of toast, buttered in the oven, and instant Maxwell House coffee. Upon hearing her shuffling through the kitchen, I get up too, and she makes me the same toast, and we sit together at the table perusing the paper—me, the Sports section; she, the Society columns—while I sip my juice and she, her coffee. We have the paper to ourselves at least until 8:00 when my Dad, who allows himself this one morning to sleep "late," drags himself into the breakfast room and takes over the entire paper, for he pays the bill.

And though they barely speak to each other, Nanny and my Dad will be in the house together all Sunday morning as my Mother eventually gathers herself, my little brother, and me and sweeps us all away to Sunday school at 9:40. Nanny might start our noon meal, though most of that chore remains for my Mother to nurture when we arrive home at 11. Sometimes Nanny works on one of her oil paintings while we're gone. Her easel is situated in her bedroom just to the side of her 12-inch black and white TV. As she paints on these Sunday mornings, she is accompanied by the dulcet strains of the famous Oklahoman faith-healer Oral Roberts, or the life lessons provided by morality plays such as "A Lamp Unto Thy Feet." Sometimes before we leave I join her in her room, especially if one of her other shows—maybe Wally Fowler— is airing Gospel Music, the only part of religious service that I truly like. I know early on and forever that Nanny's all-time favorite religious anthem is "How Great Thou Art" sung by Tennessee Ernie Ford, Mahalia Jackson, or even "Gomer Pyle" himself, Jim Nabors.

Nanny is our guiding Sunday morning spirit, and never on any of those mornings do we make it out of the house until she inspects our attire. Of course my Mother dresses us in our best Sunday suits—wool in the winter, cotton or polyester in the other months. When I am four or five, I wear snap-on bow ties. I remember clearly when I finally graduate to hook-on straight ties at age eight. So impressed with myself, these ties make going to Sunday school almost pleasurable. Satisfying Nanny's inspection is a true rite of passage—a way my Mother can keep Nanny invested in our paths and a way Nanny can remain central to ours.

I think now about how rapidly over the next few years I truly begin passing through Nanny's room, in and out her doors with just a wisp of a kiss accompanied by her lamentations about my Beatle-bangs and sneakers. My goodbyes become fleeting and then non-existent, though I never fail to appear nightly for her benedictive kiss on my forehead. Never fail, that is, until one night I awaken to find her being led from her bedroom by my parents, and by the family doctor who still makes calls in the dead of night. I can only sense what's happening as Nanny halts the progress, reaches her arms out to me, and says "There's my darlin'." The next moment, it's like none of this has happened, and I'm in my bed again.

I do at least visit my Nanny in the nursing home where she spends her last weeks. At first, she doesn't seem so changed—her decline being gradual and slow. Once when we're there, she manages to slide down her bed.

"Look at my progress," she says with pride.

That amuses my Mother, it seems, and she agrees that indeed, progress is being made. Nanny has always amused my mother, just as a child finds ways to amuse her parents. And for all the years we've been together, Nanny has seemed to me to be my mother's child, subject to the household rules of governance just as my brother and I are. And I believe that's how my mother has seen it too, which is maybe why my Nanny spends so much time at the church—why it's the one place in which she most longs to be.

There finally comes a point when Mom refuses to allow me to accompany her to the nursing home. My Nanny has experienced several strokes and surely has undergone a dramatic change.

"I don't want you to see her like that."

Maybe Mom is right. She's been protecting me from so much all my life: Advising me to eat my vegetables and to wear my cap with ear flaps in the winter wind; warning me against accepting rides from strangers and to never, ever, ride my bike in the street. But I am almost fifteen when Nanny dies, just two days before my birthday. Rightly or wrongly, my Mom's protection—though it keeps me from seeing my Nanny as a virtual corpse—denies me the chance to say goodbye to her. Worse, it ensures that I'll regret all the days when I ran so quickly out of the doors of our home-life, forgetting the good-bye that both of us wanted.

Seasonal rituals pass, and I begin attending MYF, lured not by the evening meals or the Youth Choir, but by the teenage girls who actually like my Beatle Bangs. No single lady takes Nanny's place in the kitchen now, and often the MYF supper is delivered from the nearby "Kentucky Fried Chicken." Once, Ross McIntyre offers fifteen dollars to anyone who'll drink the entire container of KFC gravy. No one is quite that stupid, but then no one supervises us very closely either. And so no Church Lady intervenes as Ross himself drains the container of semi-brown viscous fluid.

Christmas comes, and so does Easter. Though I miss Nanny, particularly on Sunday mornings as I read the comics and other news alone, buttering my toast just the way she did, it's on Mother's Day that I truly feel the strangeness of the empty space at the table, the life that's gone out of our house.

Every Mother's Day, tradition has it that you wear a tiny red rose on your lapel if your mother is still alive, a white one if she is not. I remember my Mother telling me of this tradition, as she wore her own red rose pin. And so on that first Mother's Day without Nanny, the red rose Mom has always worn has now turned white, and for the first time since she died, I hide in the bathroom and allow myself to cry for my Nanny.

Fortunately, my mind has stored other images, amusing if not healing movie reels and snapshots of my most memorable church lady.

Like this one: The summer that our next-door neighbor, Nancy Fisher, married her long-time steady, Jim Franklin. They wed in our church, and my brother, who must have been five that summer, is their ring-bearer, though the silken pillow he carries during the ceremony is only ceremonial. Someone, most likely Nancy's grandfather Oscar—aka "The Minute-Man"—has brought a super-8 camera to film the event. Weeks after the wedding, Nancy's family invites us over to watch this home-movie on a makeshift screen they set up in their den.

As the film rolls, there we all are at the reception in our church's basement, happy as the bride and groom cut their cake.

Almost as if he were trying to emulate the French New Wave cinema-verite auteurs, The Minute-Man sweeps his camera over the crowd, zooming in on well-wishers; unsteadily tracking lovely women across the crowded room. In the midst of it all, though, I notice only the Grandmothers, for they are truly everywhere at once: Sipping "frozen" green punch, holding on to their husbands (if alive), and eyeing the bride with appreciation and longing. And out of this throng, out of Miss Pridmore, and Miss Ruthie, Miss Pauline Jones and Miss Ora Latham, and even out of Mary Morey Moore (The Gargoyle), there walks my Nanny, bottled Coke in hand. She passes through the crowd, everyone watching and acknowledging her. She seems headed in a certain direction, to a previously agreed-upon destination. And then, on some silent cue, she notices the camera. She stops, looks right at it as the frame itself freezes. Is she confused, dismayed, or irritated? Does she wonder, "What is that thing doing in my Church?"

Or is she searching for me, wondering where I've gone? Wondering for the millionth time on the frozen frame that surely faded to celluloid red ages ago, what I have done with my life, why I left the Church and my other grandmothers so abruptly and finally? And most of all, why I left her?

Today, of course, I'm even farther away from remembering which Bible story/lesson derives from which book, chapter, or verse. I know neither the nuances of the synoptic gospels, the central presence in that Book of Judges, nor who Samuel, James, Uriah, and Levi actually are. So the teachings of the Church fathers are lost to me. But I know my Grandmothers, and I remember their lessons; I remember who they are by Name, by Face, and by Place. They continue to call to me, too, and are surely disappointed when I choose not to hear; when I, as usual, skip a few steps, or fail to appear.

Heads held high, eyes blinking away all that they don't want to see, they extend their hands to correct or save me. Or just to hold mine for another moment on a summer morning, or in the middle of the night when I awaken suddenly, feeling that I'm missing something important: Some vital life lesson. Despite my mistakes, their eyes continue watching me, in whatever location I sojourn to; in whatever upper room I dwell.

6
Neither the Season, Nor the Time

You might as well say it was winter, that Thanksgiving week-end when Buford was shot. It felt like late December, looked like early February: bleak pale skies, dead trees. When you looked out of our den windows at night, confronted by the darkness of those trees silhouetted against a lighter, grayer, dark-toned sky, you felt small; you felt glad to be warming against the electric wall heater or the floorboard register, and you wished your house were fully carpeted. But who had such luxuries in my small town in the mid-1960's? I had a heavy car-coat with a hood, not exactly peer-enviable material, but because of past earaches, strep throats, and my mother's built-up fears, I couldn't leave the house even for five minutes without "bundling up."

In the Alabama of my childhood, every winter we had snow. There's a picture of my Dad and me, 1961, and the snow is up to my waist, at least two feet. I know that's nothing compared to places like Nebraska, or the dreaded North. But I'm describing the Deep South, the Sun Belt, the Heart of Dixie, and I'm telling you that in those years, the winters were harsh; they lasted a full three months, and through the early 70's you could always count on that season living up to its reputation.

Today, even further north in my adopted state of South Carolina, there's at least a 40% chance that you can go outside and linger in shorts and a t-shirt on Thanksgiving and even Christmas Day. So yes, I do believe in global warming.

But global warming has nothing to do with Buford who didn't live long enough to really understand what unseasonal temperatures felt like. So on a wintry Saturday night, two days after we celebrated another American anniversary of two groups—Pilgrims, Indians—that, though we studied them in school and dressed like them for all-school assemblies, none of us ever really understood, Buford White, emerging from an A&P grocery on Carolina Avenue, was gunned down by a very distraught man. A man, or so the story goes, whose wife had just left him. But why such a bereaved and unstable man would be stalking the entrance to an A&P at 6 pm on the Saturday after Thanksgiving in 1967, no one could say then. And now, hardly anyone remembers this horror at all.

We know he had a gun, and Buford happened by. Maybe he walked too close. Maybe as he struggled with his bags Buford even bumped into the man. In Bessemer, Alabama, at this period, a Black man who bumped into a white man even in broad daylight, even under the warmth and beauty of a May sun, had better have apologized and quick.

A Black man at dusk in late fall or what is passing for winter who bumps into a white man with a gun, however...well, I hope Buford had a chance to say, or at least think, "Bless me Lord." For no apology would do. There wouldn't be a chance.

The white man emptied his gun into Buford's body. Actually, I don't know how many bullets he fired, how many penetrated poor old Buford's head, or lungs, or heart. What I heard, though, was that when the grocery bags dropped, cans of Campbell's Chicken Noodle soup and several oranges rolled to the curb. Goods meant for someone at home, someone sick maybe, but then, I don't remember anything about Buford's family; I don't know who was left waiting for him or who got that phone call later in the night after Buford had been rushed to Bessemer General. After he was pronounced dead.

I assume that the doctors there did everything they could for this man. This Black man. Of course, in regards to Buford, it's much too late for assumptions, or even hope. And it may have been too much back then.

We got a phone call that evening from our church secretary and good friend, Mary Morey Moore. It seems to me now that I actually heard her yelling through the phone lines, though more likely it was Nanny, my grandmother, who, through her own shock and distress, reported those words to us:

"Buford's been shot! In front of the A&P. They rushed him to the hospital, but he's dead!"

Simple words really and no different from what I've already told you. But at age eleven, they penetrated me, at least for that night and the next morning when it felt like our church had a hole in its white stone side.

But what penetrates me now is the realization that at this time and place, and at no other childhood time and place that I can think of, a white woman in Bessemer, Alabama, called another white woman in town and cried with her over the phone about a Black man who had been shot and killed by a white man.

At this time of my life, I believe I knew only three Black men: Elijah, our across-the-street neighbors' handy-man who conked his hair and dyed it red; Jesse, a man who cleaned floors and delivered goods for the jewelry store where my father was employed, and who "The Boss" called "Boy" even when Jesse was in his 50's; and Buford.

Buford worked at our church, a fixture as sturdy and certain as our minister back then, Dr. Sansbury. Buford had one black eye and one faded blue eye. Normally, an eye like that would have terrified me, and I do confess to staring at it more than I should have. But I was never terrified of Buford who smiled too often, who always bent down to us, shook our hands, laughed at our antics, and made sure to make us feel at home in the church. Our church. And, of course, he knew our names. All the kids' names: Jimbo, Karen, Ramona, Lynn, Freddy, and even Willie, whose parents referred to Buford as "one of the good niggers."

Naturally, all the kids loved Buford for who he was as much as because we *could* call him by his first name—the name everyone told us to call him.

I remember one of the times Buford stopped in to see Nanny; she was a fixture at the church, too, hosting banquets and WSCS meetings. Buford loved her and dropped in to see her on many occasions, often being invited to stay for lunch. On this occasion, our house was being renovated, though rather badly, by contractor Joe Ray Kurtts. Joe Ray had replaced a windowsill in my bedroom, but it was askew, so he had to return and make it right. Buford, being in the wrong place at the wrong time, was enlisted to help, or knowing Buford, he most likely volunteered. In any case, as Joe Ray was re-nailing the window with massive blows that felt more like he was trying to split wood, he missed his mark and the nail flew up, right into Buford's eye. This incident makes me think now of the Faulkner character "Anse Bundren," who not-even-ironically remarks about his "misfortunate" son Cash, the victim of a wagon accident carting his dead mother's coffin to town as she lay in it dead, that at least it was the same leg he broke the previous winter. So you might say it was a bit of luck that it was Buford's faded blue eye that the nail penetrated.

Still, even a blind eye bleeds. And so Joe Ray and my mother rushed Buford to Bessemer General where, of course, this time he survived. A couple of days later when Joe Ray popped in to clean up, I remember him saying to Nanny, "I sure hate what happened to that boy." That, of course, despite the fact that Buford was a man at least ten years older than Joe Ray. I wonder if Buford had a good medical plan; if Joe Ray contributed anything. Or if my family did.

What I remember most is that Buford always dressed nicely: work clothes for weekdays, neat and pressed, and his white suit coat with a carnation, and dark pleated pants on Sundays. Just like all the other men.

On Easter Sunday, he even wore a white rose in his lapel.

He'd open the doors on those Sundays for all the ladies, make small talk with the men, and when the service started, he'd retire to the basement with the maids, where they'd sit and wait till the service was over at which time they'd either serve a banquet-style lunch or simply pack up and go to a place where they, too, could worship our Lord.

As I said, Buford loved to laugh, and he'd chase my little brother around the church basement, my brother beside himself with laughter and like as not wetting his pants in the chase. Once, my brother asked Buford to show him his muscle, his bicep, and when Buford flexed, we both stood quietly.

The A&P where Buford was shot was only a block around the corner from our church, the place where Buford was employed for over twenty-three years; from Arlington school where my brother and I went from first to sixth grade; and from Highland Bakery where I bought lemon ice cream and baseball cards during those years. Just across the railroad tracks from the A&P was a "state store," where Bessemer's citizenry bought its state-controlled liquor, and down the street a block farther was Ralph's Recreation Center where the controls, or so I hear, were much more lax.

Maybe the white man who killed Buford had been run out of Ralph's. Maybe he had been refused a bottle at the state store, which had also been robbed many times, and so run out of there. Whatever the story, he did run into Buford next, or as reality may have had it, Buford ran into him.

And so the story goes that after he pumped those bullets into a man armed only with grocery sacks, the white man then drove to neighboring Lipscomb, pulled to the side of the road, and shot himself in the head with a bullet he either accidentally or intentionally saved.

I've tried, but so far I can't find an obituary for Buford White, a Black man who once entered and became a part of my life. It seems very late to be asking such questions, but what did his life mean to me, and why wasn't I more affected by his death at the time? I don't remember stopping whatever I was doing to cry or pray or even sit silently somewhere, reflecting.

I ask my wife about this, about my lack of feeling.

"Are you kidding," she asks. "How old were you? Eleven? Eleven-year olds can't process this information. They don't know how they feel. You were affected, though. Look at what you remember and how long you've remembered it."

It's true. I think that on the weekend Buford was murdered, Alabama beat Auburn 7-3 on a rainy, freezing afternoon. I remember that my Dad attended the game. With the flu. Alabama won on a last-minute forty-plus yard run by quarterback Kenny Stabler. "The Snake." It's famous in Alabama lore, and after the game, Dad came home and went to bed with a 103-degree fever. So yeah, I might have been focused on other, seemingly important life events.

And in the end, how can, how an eleven-year old process his first murder?

To help me process and remember, I have found that the Board of Bessemer's First Methodist Church passed and printed a resolution in the *Methodist Christian Advocate* honoring Buford. That resolution remembers him as having "the qualities of a Christian gentleman," and it praises him for his years of service to the church during a time when he couldn't actually attend its services; when his children, if he did indeed have some, couldn't attend Arlington school. The resolution thanks God for letting "us" have Buford for all those years, and it says "his labors will long be remembered."

For how long were they? No one, to my knowledge, can accurately say. It's funny, but just the other night as I was trying to prod a longtime family friend's memory of Buford, she said,

"It's just so sad, but no one remembers these things much anymore." She remembered Buford, though she didn't remember that he had been murdered. "I did go to his funeral, though," and then she suggested others who might be able to help.

"Your mother, though, she's the one with the good memory. She's the one you should ask."

Which, of course, I already had. My mother is the one who told me about the grocery bags, the distraught man who later killed himself. But when you're dealing with memory, you have to keep prodding. So I called her again, asked her other questions: did Buford have a family? Did the church do anything for his family? How do you suppose Mary Morey Moore learned of his death? My mother didn't know the answer to the last question, but of the other two:

"Yes, I think Buford did have a wife and several kids. Five or six maybe. I think the oldest son was named after Buford, too. I'm sure the church did something for them. It's too bad your Nanny isn't alive; she would have known more. Or Jason Dean; he could have told you."

"OK, Mom, but quit naming other dead people."

"I know, I know. I went to Buford's funeral, though, down there on Ninth Avenue at one of the Black churches. Most of our church went, too. In fact, there were more white people there than Black."

I had no memory of a funeral or that anyone from my family went. But I'm glad to know this. It helps in a way I can't explain.

"And you know, I remember Buford telling me once that he preferred the services at the white folks' church to those at the Black folks' church."

"Do you think he ever sat in the sanctuary for our services?"

"Well, I don't know. I don't think so. But maybe he sat up in the balcony or walked around in the back."

Now I really had something to think about. I know how badly the congregation acted when our minister welcomed a Black family to morning service a few years after Buford died. Some threatened to have the preacher fired if he ever did something like that again. I remember driving home that day with one of my friends. I remember him calling our preacher "a nigger lover." And I remember how this friend always seemed so nice to Buford.

Was it just that Buford was "ours?"

At that memory, I once again see Buford's face before me:

"Mom, do you know how Buford got that bad eye?"

"No, I don't."

"Do you remember when Joe Ray Kurtts mishit the nail and it flew into Buford's bad eye?"

"No, I don't remember that either. But I do remember this: Buford was an orphan, and he was raised by a white family."

"Oh my God, where, in Bessemer?"

"No, in some little town not too far away. Maybe Uniontown, but I really don't know."

I figure Buford was in his forties or fifties when he died, so that means he was raised sometime in the 1920's or earlier. By a white family. And I'm supposing now that I'll never know whether his surname was actually "White," or if it was the name of the white family that raised him.

"How could that have happened," my wife asks.

"Well," I say, "you know that for every rule there's an irony, a contradiction."

"A rebel," she says.

"Yes, a rebel."

This, too, pleases me. I don't want things to be so one-sided, so clear-cut, so "Black and White." Even in Bessemer.

Honestly, I do know many people who, if you ask them, remember Buford fondly, in the old way. The church we attended those many Sundays and where Buford worked and gave so much of his time, his life, closed down in 2007. It was in such a state of disrepair, and the congregation had dwindled to maybe twenty or thirty worshippers. My mother told me, too, that Buford once said that our church wouldn't have made it back in the forties if it weren't for Mr. Bradley—a wealthy member of the Board—supporting it.

The things a custodian knows.

But whatever Buford thought, our longtime family friend said, "When Buford was killed, I thought that the backbone of the church died too. I wondered if we'd survive." But they did for another forty years until they sold the church to, I hear, a Black congregation.

Today, if you look in the drawers of the few worshippers who are left, the ones who moved on to another congregation, you might find one of the church's old paper-glossy yearbooks. And if you look under "Custodial Staff" in those years, the 1950's and 60's, you'll see Buford standing in his white coat next to the various maids and babysitters. All of them Black, and all very nameless. All very dark and unknown.

7
Searching for Higher Ground

The empty, Sunday afternoon mall parking lot where I learn to drive in the summer of 1972 offers no challenges really. So after I complete a series of uncomplicated turns around mammoth poles of artificial light, Mom suggests that I drive us home. Taking "the back way," through poor and segregated neighborhoods, we pass our maid Dissie's house. I toot the horn and wave to her as she sits on her front porch. I see her full-face smile, her gold-encased upper-front tooth twinkling in the sunlight.

After a few months of accident-free, licensed driving in my own neighborhood, Mom allows me to run errands for her. One of these is to drive Dissie home on Saturday afternoons.

Grabbing Mom's keys and making sure my wallet is tucked safely in my back jeans pocket, I race to the front door:

"Dissie! You ready to go?"

"I'm comin' Bob (her nickname for me). Just let me get my bag."

I escort her to our '67 Tempest, a two-door model. Opening the passenger-side door, I wait for Dissie to settle in so that I can close it securely behind her.

Dissie is a big-thighed, big-hipped woman, and quite round on top. She's getting older, though I refuse to allow her age to sink in fully. I think she's as young and energetic as she's ever been, though I clearly see the evidence that our windows and floors are not quite as shiny as they were when I was a kid. She still sings in low, soft tones as she works, and her laugh is still as contagious as ever when she recounts Lucy's and Ethel's escapades on the morning reruns.

I love Dissie. And I believe I'd do anything for her.

I'm excited for us to drive through the streets of Bessemer now. We can talk, listen to the hits on WVOK. What a feeling—Dissie beside me—me driving her home!

As my vision crystallizes, though, Dissie does the one thing I never expect: she pushes back the front seat and climbs in the back.

"Dissie, you don't..."

But she does.

We drive on to her house in silence, WVOK playing songs that I no longer can remember.

II

I was a kid who never pretended, never hid my true feelings. When my family supported JFK in the 1960 national election, one of my closest friends scoffed that Kennedy was nothing but a "nigger-lover." My silent mouth gaped as low and open as a gutted deer. Embarrassed, slightly ashamed, I didn't know what to say, what this meant.

When my parents told me two years later to "Act naturally" around the first Black children to integrate our elementary school, and to speak to them only if spoken to first, I felt even more confused. I already talked naturally to Black people: our maid and baby-sitters, Dissie, Georgia, and Mona Lee; the custodians of our church, Buford, Linnis, and Eugenia. When Dissie brought her nieces, nephews, and granddaughter to our house, I not only spoke to them naturally, like the friends they were, but I also played all my games with them: Parcheesi, Old Maid, whiffle-ball, and touch football.

My first thought about my parents' command was that they meant "be polite," which I normally was. But I knew something else was occurring. Their faces looked worried sometimes, even afraid. These looks reminded me of their other warnings like: "Don't ever get in the car with someone you don't know," or "Don't take candy from a stranger!"

So on my first day of school integration, as Dad sits waiting in the car to drive me to my destiny at our neighborhood school, my mother, still in her gown, and my grandmother, bottle of Coke in hand, send me off with this magic formula:

"You just mind your own business, and they'll mind theirs. Then there won't be any trouble. And if one of them does start trouble, you march right to the principal's office and tell *him* what happened."

Start trouble? What sort of trouble, I wondered? Yet, I never asked. Besides, wouldn't going to the principal betray a code? The code not to snitch or tattle? I'm standing on strange ground now, not sure where to step, how to keep a level head.

How to survive in this particular integrated sea.

In those strange and anxious times, I believe I did the best I could. Since I didn't know any of these new Black students at all, I treated them during school hours as I did any unknown kid: I said nothing to them but kept an eye out for them.

I guess I was acting naturally then.

During that first year of integration in Bessemer, as I was tossing myself spiral passes one afternoon in my front yard, a Black boy named Brown Chapman came riding down our street on his banana-seated, high-handled bike. As he rode closer, I watched him steadily. Then, he lifted his left hand:

"Hi Terry."

Though stunned at the recognition, I waved back:

"Hi Brown."

"See you tomorrow."

"Yeah, see ya."

Wow. Talking to a relatively unknown Black kid was actually

OK. Nothing "troubling" happened to either of us. I wanted to tell my family about this friendly encounter. But I didn't. And I was also glad that none of my neighborhood friends witnessed this exchange. It might have been the end of me in my struggle to be just one of the gang.

For when my "gang" used the word "Nigger," I said nothing. I stayed silent on my own home grounds. I valued safety above all other considerations.

Though I knew my world was shifting, I also knew that the one constant was Dissie. She arrived on these sunny mornings of my childhood with a smile that warmed me more than the heat rising from the floor register I'd hover over on winter days. As she held me, I could hear my parents welcoming Dissie, their own warmth, I thought, matching mine.

This was love, truly, and I thought then that I understood the feeling well—that it would never alter or die, just like a porch light on a crisp autumn football Friday night.

III

"We'll park at Dissie's house," Daddy says as we drive toward the stadium. I am six years old, in the first grade, and this will be my first Bessemer High School football game.

Her porch light is on for us as we pull into the dried-ruts of her front-yard driveway. She's usually in bed by seven, she says, but on these autumn Friday nights of my childhood, she waits by her door, for us.

"Hey Mistah Alvin! Hey Bob!"

"Dissie!" And I dash up the unpainted porch steps into her shining brown arms. She's changed her soft gray uniform for a blue flowered house-dress, but her laughing eyes are my constant.

"Is ya'll ready for the game? It ought to be a good one. Billy and Nelly Ann's going. They say those folk from Phillips is mighty rough."

"Hey Dissie," my Dad says. "Yeah, but I think Bessemer's ready for 'em. You oughta come watch too."

"No sir. I'se gettin' in the bed, but I be listnin' to Mistah Porter on the radio."

She lets go of me then after an extra squeeze.

"Now you be good and mind yo Daddy, hear?"

"Sure I will Dissie. And I'll root 'em in for you! You're comin' tomorrow morning aren't you?"

"Shore am, ifn the Good Lawd willin'! Nita'll be comin' too!"

"Oh boy, I can show her my new football!"

"She'll love that...Now you give me a hug an' go on with Mistah Alvin."

"OK, see you in the morning!"

Dissie lives only a block from the showplace high school stadium constructed out of brick and mortar in the 1930s and planted in the middle of the black section of Bessemer: Eight square blocks of unpainted, rundown houses, many of which did not offer indoor plumbing on the west side of town. In the ensuing decades, Bessemer High School rewarded the town's investment by winning six or eight state championships, all before the early 1960s. And during these decades the attending faithful parked everywhere, including in the yards of the ramshackle houses dotting 4th Avenue, just across the street from the heralded stadium entrance.

Dissie's house, as Dad described it, was the archetypal southern "shotgun shack," an untreated clapboard, but I didn't care. The inside of Dissie's house comforted me, for it was as neat and clean as those of many of the White families I more regularly frequented. Her bed was always made, the furniture was aligned with the room, and all chairs were politely pushed under their respective tables. The several shaded lamps on these tables softened, diffused, the harsh overhead light. Maybe it was that quality of muted light, along with the comforting scent of Dissie, that warmed my soul whenever I set foot inside her door and that made me ask to spend the night there: A request that I made earlier that afternoon:

"Dissie, can I please come spend the night with you?"

"Honey, you know Miss Jo Ann need you here to help with yo little brother!"

"But she has Daddy and Nanny—can't I go with you?"

Dissie's laughing eyes roll a bit then over at my mother who always referred to me as "Buddy."

"Now Buddy, don't bother Dissie. She's worked hard all week tending to you and Mike. She's tired and needs her rest. You'll see her tomorrow morning, so don't bother her anymore."

I heard her tone more than her words. The pitch was high, and if I didn't mind her then, another, higher pitch would lead to yelling, maybe even to a "switching." What was so different about these two places, I wondered? But I never asked anyone. Intimidated by my mother's tone, I knew instinctively that to ask her would put me on shaky ground. Yet, I didn't understand what was wrong. Sure, Dissie's house wasn't as large or as nice as ours.

But it was hers!

And Dissie loved me. She took care of me in our home, so why wouldn't she in hers?

The best I could do was to step inside Dissie's house for a minute or two—one more moment with the woman who was like a mother to me. She might even take me inside for a piece of her homemade lemon pound cake.

But the game finally had a stronger pull. I took my Daddy's sure, strong hand, both to ease my sadness at leaving Dissie and to ensure that in the ensuing crowds, I would never lose my connection to him. As we walked away, Dissie stood on her porch watching us. Several times I'd turn back to wave to her. Dissie never waved just her hand, however; her entire arm flagged me in a way similar to highway utility men giving the "All Clear" signal. As we peaked the slight incline that would take us down to the stadium entrance, I stole one last look at her. One last wave, and then she disappeared.

And then Daddy and I entered the stadium and found our seats, secure in the comfort of our familiar surroundings.

As hard as it was leaving Dissie, the minute Daddy and I took our seats I was *his* boy, relishing each play under his protective care. We cheered together for Bessemer, and I hoped that one day he might be watching me take my place on this field and catch the winning touchdown pass.

During time-outs, I'd take in all the fans cheering with us.

"Daddy, where do you think Billy and Nelly Ann are sitting?"

"Oh, over there in the end zone, see?"

And he pointed to the rickety, unpainted bleachers of the West end zone. There somewhere among the darker hues were Billy and Nelly Ann.

"Can I go over and say Hi later?"

"No, you better stay up here with me. You might get lost."

The fear of getting lost was primal for me, so I didn't question him. It was good enough to know they were there, enjoying the game as I was. Of course, it hadn't hit me yet that though they yelled for Bessemer High, they were forbidden from attending it.

Sitting with my daddy high in the home stands, I didn't think about who could or couldn't go to certain schools. I didn't wonder what Billy or Nelly Ann or their friends thought about their seats in the stadium or their perspective on the sights in front of them. It all seemed so natural to me—our separate places.

And, of course, I never doubted that had I been allowed to go see them there, they would have been delighted to see me.

What they couldn't see or know was the moment when the man sitting next to me—a friend of my father's who would one day be my Sunday School teacher—tapped me on the shoulder and pointed to those west end zone bleachers:

"Look! There are our *other* fans!"

"Yeah," I said. And then I laughed with him. For what else could I do?

Except feel my shame—the shame of envisioning Dissie in her clean and tidy home just two blocks away listening on the radio to the cheers of Bessemer High's mainly white fans, and knowing that I had just chosen another side.

The game ended in a tie, 13-13, but Dad and I left the stadium a few minutes before the final gun to get a head start on the post-game traffic. When we reached Dissie's place, everything looked the same: the car, Dissie's house, except that the inside lights were off. On the way home, I tried to believe that everything was the same, that nothing really had changed for me that night. That nothing would ever change *in* my world.

And maybe it hadn't. For as usual, Dissie had left her porch light on for us: a light that in my imagination kept on burning through that night, long after we had driven away and I was safely tucked into my own bed, where I'd fall asleep, dreaming of the morning when I would be back in her arms again.

As blatant segregation reluctantly waned, and integration became at least a nominal reality, I grew even more uncertain about where to stand.

The separate water fountains in public spaces caused me to stumble one day, as, shopping with some family friends, I approached the fountain nearest to me:

"That's not your fountain! Yours is over there on the other side of that elevator, the one that says *White*," the mother of this family warned.

I saw the words; I just didn't know what they meant then. But I did know that Dissie drank from our tap. She used *our* bathroom too.

The public/private distinction lay beyond my grasp. And how could I question a white adult's pronouncement as to where I should or shouldn't drink? I certainly heard the tone in her voice; I saw the fear, and something else in her eyes. Today, I might call that look "disgust;" then, I knew only that if I wanted to keep playing with her son, I better obey her.

It never occurred to me either that all public spaces, before 1965—community pool, baseball fields, amusement parks—were safe grounds for me, for any white person. But not for Dissie or her children. So when I'd describe to her my thrills at Kiddie-Land, she would listen to all my stories and simply say, "I wish Billy an' Nelly Ann an' them could see it."

I never asked her why they couldn't.

And then one summer day, not even I could go anymore:

"It's being boycotted; it's too dangerous to go there now," my mother said.

Though I knew this change was somehow tied to school integration, I couldn't see how tied everything was.

How unfair our black and white world had been. How I had benefited from who I was.

I didn't want to take sides in this new place. Yet, everyone else had picked a side—one entirely based on color, leaving me standing where? Searching for what place?

IV

On that transformative first day of integration during my sixth grade year, I came to school ready to act naturally. My teacher lectured us about proper behavior under these special circumstances:

"Class, we must all be respectful of each other. I'm depending on the rest of you to set the proper example. Welcome your two new classmates like you would anyone else."

She left the room for a minute, shutting the door firmly behind her. We waited, expecting what?

"Are they boys or girls," my friend Robert asked.

"Where will they sit," a little girl named Sandra wondered.

Before anyone could answer, Miss Horton entered again, accompanied by two girls, dressed primly, neatly. They followed Miss Horton to her desk, and when she stopped, they stared only at each other.

"Class, this is Cynthia Williams and Zepora Delk. They've

come from Dunbar elementary. Now girls, your desk is right over there by the window. Go take your seats and get out your social studies books."

Cynthia and Zepora trudged to their desks, looking only at the floor in front of them and never making a sound.

Over the next few days, I tried not to stare at them or do anything to call attention to myself. But one day, passing their table on the way to sharpen my pencil, I looked down at Zepora's place and noticed that she had drawn on the back of her blue Nifty binder a Black Power insignia with those very words imbedded in the mighty black fist.

"WOW!" I remarked as I passed.

She caught my eye just long enough.

"My cousin drew that."

"OK," I replied as I found my seat and stared at my own binder which was itself emblazoned with various legends of "Alabama football," "Paul Revere and the Raiders," and boy-girl initials embraced in hearts like GTB + MJT.

What strange and misguided advice my elders gave me. If I had acted "naturally," I might have ribbed Zepora a bit for her sixth grade pretensions. If she were white, our teasing might have lasted more than a moment. It might have carried over into other days, maybe even into the sort of playful flirtation I had with my white girl friends like Mary Jane and Laurie.

If I had truly acted naturally, I might have made a new friend, created a new space. And then, what would any of us have done?

V

Throughout the increasing waves of school integration—the busing of black kids to white schools; the creation of segregated white academies often sanctioned by specific Christian denominations—I sank into my white grounds, amongst my white peers who still used terms like "nigger" and "jigaboo" naturally. But mainly, they focused more on adolescent desire to be with the "in Group" and to go to as many make-out parties as possible.

In my junior-high and high school, everything centered on my friends. On fall Friday nights, we'd meet just inside the stadium gate, and then proceed to our rightful place in the student section. Of course, though technically integrated, white students and black students did not actually intermingle, but our sections were adjoining. As far as progress went, this was the best we would do, though it didn't stop certain white students, the so-called "bleacher-bums," from bringing in an enormous rebel flag and singing "Dixie."

This was the early 1970's. What *were* we all now? Separate? Equal? Integrated? Jess Lanier High Purple Tigers?

And among the Purple Tigers now was Dissie's granddaughter, Nita, the apple of Dissie's eye. I can't begin to grasp fully, much less describe, what Dissie felt knowing the two of us were attending the same school.

"Bob, you see Nita at school, don't you?"

"Sure Dissie. We pass each other in the halls. Just the other day I saw her and asked her how she was doing. She seemed fine."

"That's good. I know it's hard when you first get there."

In summers past—long before high school or even junior high—Dissie brought Nita to our house to spend the day with my brother Mike and me.

On those summer days, we'd play Home Run Derby in our backyard, and Nita, without fail, would whomp the tar out of our pitching with arms so skinny you'd think she couldn't even lift the bat. We had such fun on those mornings, and the fact that Nita could run faster and hit harder than we could just didn't matter.

Of course I "knew" Nita was black, and certainly she "knew" I was white. We knew intuitively that in the Alabama of our youth, our relationship was sanctioned only under the roof of my house, including the back, but never the front yard.

We never opted out of playing together. Ever.

And we didn't think in terms of boyfriend/girlfriend as we moved into our teen years. That is, until one June day when Keith, my best friend, and Sandra Ann surprised us with an impromptu visit while Nita, Mike, and I were competing for home runs in the backyard. When my white friends arrived, their shock registered from their full-moon eyes to their gaping mouths. Upon seeing them, Nita, her own eyes to the ground and altogether silently, laid the bat on the board we used for home plate, and retreated inside to the kitchen, where her grandmother was rolling out the biscuit dough for our lunch. For weeks after, my two friends teased me mercilessly:

"Where's your new girlfriend? Is she coming over again on Saturday? She sure likes you!"

"Naw, my Momma made me play with her; it's not like I ever wanted to. I never *asked* her to come over!"

And after that day everything changed for us. Despite the years of our summer place together, I saw that Nita and I had never been on equal ground.

When Nita first appeared in the Jess Lanier High School hallways and we passed each other amidst our various crowds, we *did* speak to each other. Naturally, and by name. I know that's not much, and truly, I'm not boasting about it. But it was more than anyone else had, at least in my school.

We didn't always speak, but I don't think Nita and I ever failed to catch each other's eye in the two years we spent together in high school. To me, she seemed like just another normal freshman—and then sophomore—girl, walking with her friends, holding her books, eating that horrible cafeteria food: Just another black girl in those corridors who was ultimately off-limits to me. But then, I have no idea what *she* thought as we passed—how she really saw me.

Occasionally I saw Nita at football games, but by then, I had learned a new entrance to our mutual field. When I turned sixteen and got my license, my Daddy decided to let me drive to the games that year by myself. As I drove toward Bessemer Stadium, however, the charge I felt being behind the wheel of my Dad's '67 Buick Special almost lost its surge when I glanced at the vacant seat beside me where, in past days, I had sat quite happily.

And then, there was that other vacant place.

For following Daddy's lead, I started parking at the armory on the other side of the stadium from Dissie's house. I knew it wasn't right. And now I was willing to leave aside the practical reason and hear my own voice telling me this uncomfortable truth: I was avoiding the embarrassment of having any of my friends know that I parked at my maid's house. I was avoiding any potential conflict if a girl I liked or a boy I was jealous of saw me making nice to an elderly Black woman—a woman who loved me but could also embarrass me.

When I'd see her on Saturday morning, we'd discuss the game. But Dissie never raised the most troubling question:

"Why don't you park at my house any more, Bob?"

"Well, you see, I found this other place...it's closer to the stadium, and easier to beat the traffic when I leave."

By not asking, was she protecting me still? Or was it that through these decades she simply knew when to remain silent... and where to stand in the relative position of our lives?

Though I felt guilty enough, at least I didn't have to explain to anyone, certainly not Nita, what I had done—whom I had chosen to avoid.

The love I betrayed.

Because I couldn't speak to Nita at the game. School was one thing, but the stadium stands were purely social. Me, talking to a black girl at the game? I'd never hear the end of it. Worse, I might have to take a stand myself for once—might have to cross a line that I wouldn't be allowed to step back over afterward.

So I stayed on the "right" side, not understanding the consequences—not knowing how deep and lasting a betrayal can be.

Still, I noticed Nita. I saw her clearly, as she did me. I remember the night it dawned on me that she looked different from the girl I knew before. She was standing with her crowd at the bottom of the stands, and someone had a transistor radio from which a Stevie Wonder song was pulsating:

"Teachers keep on teachin'

Preachers keep on preachin'
World keep on turnin'
Cause it won't be too long
Oh no
I'm so glad that he let me try it again
Cause my last time on earth I lived a whole world of sin
I'm so glad that I know more than I knew then
Gonna keep on tryin..."

We smiled at each other before I moved on, back up the stands to some girl who was destined to desert me later that night. But I kept thinking about Nita and what was so different about her. When it finally registered in my feeble brain, I wasn't surprised, though I was a bit shocked. Beneath her pretty white top, Nita was sporting "falsies."

Not that it really mattered, I suppose, to me or any of my friends who, I'm sure, never noticed a thing despite the fact that white and black kids couldn't help but touch each other during those tentative days of early integration: The days when the stadium aisles and school corridors were simply too crowded and narrow for anyone to avoid human contact.

VI

The next spring, on one of the last Saturdays that Dissie and I had together before I graduated and moved off to college, I gave her this reassurance:

"I saw Nita at Class Day this week. She was laughing with her group of friends. I think it's been a good year for her."

To which Dissie smiled with her entire body: "She should be happy. She made A's on her report card this time. Yep, she just loves bein' in high school."

And it's only today, in my own house and as I write these very words, that I realize I have no idea what happened to the girl with those skinny brown arms, my summer "girlfriend." My place in the world allowed me to leave her behind, to believe I could simply forget her.

Which, of course, isn't nearly as bad as what we all did to Dissie.

My mother tells me now that we let Dissie go because Dissie's daughter finally demanded that she be paid at least a minimum wage and that we also cover her health care. Apparently, my Dad balked at this. We were already paying her social security, plus her weekly wage: fifteen dollars for the four days she worked per week. Days that averaged eight hours. So in a phone message early one morning, my Mom reluctantly told Dissie not to come back. And that was that.

That was our secret. We detested George Wallace, supported public schools. We didn't use the word "nigger." But we didn't believe in an open social mixing of the races. There were no good, convincing grounds for our convictions—our familial stance. Except survival amongst our "own kind."

I know that in the aftermath of Dissie's dismissal, I moved on all-too-quickly and completely, abandoning all my old feelings for this woman who never showed me anything but love.

Still, the past has a way of waving to you from old porches.

My wife and I are visiting my parents and are driving home one afternoon from Bessemer's mall. I'm pointing out the old sites as we pass when I spot Dissie sitting on the porch of her daughter's house, just around the corner from her former home. I slow down, park the car, and then we mount the steps to Dissie who is now nearly blind. At first she is cautious, even a bit apprehensive of these shadows emerging toward her. But then she hears my voice:

"Dissie, it's Bob."

"Oh...now I just knew it was you!"

I introduce these two women: the one still very dark and now so wrinkled; the other olive-skinned with deep ebony hair. Dissie hugs both of us, and we make our own variety of small talk. And then it's time to go. But as we're leaving, she gives me one last smile, the one that lit my entire world so long ago:

"I'm glad to see you so happy, Bob!"

Then she waves to me as if I'm only going to a game, as if in another few hours she'll be seeing me again, at our house in the morning.

As if the years betrayed nothing in us, even though we both know they did.

8
Colored Memories

Somewhere in the autumn of first grade, Mrs. Baird hands out an outlined page for us to color. It's a scene in a neighborhood much like ours. A tree-lined block, and as you gaze down that sidewalk you notice a little girl coming your way. She's holding her schoolbooks flat against her chest, as girls do. You can't quite see the details of her face, but in my mind she's smiling. Her long hair hangs behind her in a ponytail. Leaves are falling to the ground, and in the distance, a school bus heads away from the school and away from our girl, leaving her alone and ripe for the taking. Her parents must trust her. They must have read all the safety rules to her. And they must think nothing bad could possibly happen in their quaint little community.

I often walked home too, but never alone, at least not until third grade when I knew better how to stay on the straightest path, the direct route up 19th street, five blocks to home. On the milder first grade afternoons, five of us would walk home together: Mary Jane, Laurie, Randy, Ted and me. It was the fall of 1962, and it seems impossible now to think back to that time and consider all that was about to happen in Alabama, in the South. In our nation.

But back to our coloring scene. As the girl gets closer we can see, though she can't, someone else watching her. A man on the left lurking behind an enormous oak tree. You might call him a harbinger of all that will befall us in the coming years. He's a white man. His uncolored face has the blackest eyes I've ever seen. Does he even have eyeballs, and if so, how do I color them? He's hiding but ready for his chance, which is approaching as surely as all the days and weeks of our coming holiday season. As hidden as he is for this moment, he's hiding something even deeper behind his back.

A bag with the word "Candy" written on it.

Mrs. Baird explains to us that the picture is trying to teach us something:

"Never accept candy from a stranger, and never go with someone you don't know even if they seem nice and say they know you. This little girl doesn't know this man. Do you think she'll take his candy? Would you?"

When Mrs. Baird finishes, we begin our coloring. Blue skies, red and gold leaves, green or brown grass depending on how observant we are of our father's yard work. But when it gets to the bag of candy, our views diverge sharply. Some color it blue-violet, others brick red, and still others completely black.

Brenda Sue Stokes, however, pulls the yellow-orange Crayola from her pack of sixty-four. When we finish, it is her bag that stands out amongst all the others, a phosphorescence that eventually wins her first prize in the Responsible Citizen Coloring Contest. Her drawing will hang on the wall outside the principal's office the rest of the year.

The funny thing is that though I never would accept candy from a stranger, because of the color she used, because of the perfect way she kept that color within those candy bag lines leaving the word as clear and prominent as before, I want that bag of candy. I want to grab it and open it and eat everything inside. It scares me a little bit how badly I want that bag.

In these years, I never hear of any kid getting taken by a

stranger. I wonder now *if* our parents would have told us, or *what* they would have told us if one of us had gone missing, stolen. For what can you tell a six-year old about abuse, torture, and rape? About vulnerability and things that can happen if you aren't cautious and careful?

About what can happen when you walk home alone.

Or when you ride a bicycle against cautioning lights, bells, or whistles.

II

It's true that kids don't always listen to their teacher's lessons. Thinking back on it now, I don't know why our teachers didn't ask us to color a new picture every day given how many dangers and predators and things there are that go screaming through the night, or mid-afternoon.

We could have colored a beach scene with gulls flying overhead. After a picnic lunch, little Mary might want to jump back into the ocean, but her pretty mommy asks her politely to sit by her and make a sand castle for an hour or so until her food digests.

Or a scene of a pleasant neighborhood with storm clouds hovering, and a particular funnel-looking cloud about to descend on a boy and his mom as they try to take groceries out of the trunk of their station wagon.

Or a scene of a city street with a friendly policeman on the corner blowing his whistle to prevent Susie and Freddy from crossing against the light.

Or maybe this scene:

A double train track running right through the center of town. Its guardrails are descending, the red lights flashing, and four blocks away to the left, the engine of the Southern Railroad line bears down, horn blaring for all it's worth. It's heading to Nashville, maybe carrying coal or warehouse goods or new building materials. It has certainly slowed a bit, but since it's not stopping in this little town, it's still moving at 40-50 mph. Of course everyone else stops: the cars, the pedestrians, even old crazy Joe with his steering wheel. We'll never know, however, why one boy on a bicycle doesn't, why he tries to beat that train. Is he running late on his newspaper delivery route? Is he showing off? Does he enjoy living dangerously? Or does he sincerely believe he can glide between the wooden guard rails and slip past the moving hunk of iron and metal?

This would have been a coloring lesson to consider. Who knows whether any of us would have heeded it, or remembered it a few years later when it should have mattered to this nine-year old boy? Surely, you say, we got the message about waiting for trains from our parents, teachers, society at large, and I suppose we did. I know I did, though I have to confess that even now in my late fifties, when I hear the train-horn or see the guardrails lowering, I wonder if I can beat it. And if I believe I can, I do.

But on April 8, 1967, I was ten, and Terry Blaine Wenndt was only nine. One grade ahead of him, I knew him only as another fourth grader, another face in the hallway, another body running over the playground.

Another ghostly presence in the world of pre-adolescence.

I remember him vividly only through the photograph I saw in the paper the week after the accident. A photo of a butch-cut, blonde, smiling boy who looked as normal as he could be. What wasn't normal, though, was the way he'll always be remembered: as a headless torso, bloodied and mangled and dead for no reason.

I heard all sorts of things after the fact: his head was completely severed, his legs too. His torso was dragged for three city blocks. The engineer saw him but couldn't stop that speeding train. Much later I'll hear that he tried to beat the train, that his front tire got caught in the rail groove, that he didn't want to leave his bike behind. How can anyone know these things? What evidence remains? What else can we do but wonder, and talk about it?

April 8, 1967. In the days before the accident we were listening as the double-sided hit "Penny Lane/Strawberry Fields Forever" released itself "there beneath [our] blue suburban skies." Such a happy tune. Just over a year to the day later, we are mourning or in some cases celebrating [for this IS Alabama] when Dr. King is assassinated in Memphis on a cold and cloudy day.

What is the matter with April?

It ushers in the timeless season of baseball, yet it's also the "cruelest month." It brings the "showers" so necessary for "May flowers." It contains both Hitler's birthday and Holocaust Remembrance Day. And Tax Day. It began the Civil War and ended Lincoln's life. It finds itself at the very beginning of Chaucer's semi-fictional pilgrimage; usually at the ending of "Our Lord's" time on earth; and fully incorporating the Angel of Death's passing over the houses of the enslaved Israelites.

In 2011, April 27 brought a series of deadly tornados through Tuscaloosa, Alabama, and near my mother's house in Bessemer. I was with her on that day. It felt like a day at the beach at first: balmy and increasingly windy. Unwisely we stayed in the area instead of driving north and far away to complete safety. A day earlier I had visited the scene of a similar tornado that passed through several years before. The 2011 tornado traveled that very same path, mercifully sparing our house. These events, of course, are entirely natural.

April 2014. More tornados, veering slightly northeast of their familiar path. Again, my mother's house isn't damaged, though a piece of aluminum the size of a Toyota Corolla lodges itself in a front oak tree. Two blocks away, both houses and trees are uprooted. The path diagonally dissects the older part of town. I have no information on deaths or injuries, but I know that the tornado's path leads it right over the spot where Terry Wenndt tried to cross a double train track forty-seven years earlier to the month.

April 7, 1967, my father celebrates his forty-first birthday. My mother makes his favorite banana pudding in lieu of cake. We are all carefree and happy. As maybe the Wenndt family was on this night. The night before their lives were so unnaturally torn.

III

When I begin my research, I don't know the right year of the accident. I contact the Birmingham Public Library, but they see no record of such an accident in 1962, the year I think it must have happened. I contact the Bessemer Library by email, but they never reply to my query. I tell my frustrations to my brother Mike, and it's he who first alerts me that my memory isn't as precise as I think:

"The boy's name was Terry Wenndt, and he had an older bother named Randy. I was in the car with Mom, and we had to drive near the scene. I remember seeing a lot of cars and the train stopped somewhere between 18th and 19th streets. We knew something bad had happened."

"I must not have been with you," I say, for surely I would have remembered." Did y'all stop?"

"No, Momma didn't want to. But I think I was in the first grade with his younger brother Timmy."

Which would have made me a fifth grader.

Mike's memory is like those ice skating blades spewing shards of rink when the Olympian lands after a triple axle. I have no doubt he's right.

Next, I call my childhood friend Joe.

"You probably won't know what I'm talking about, but do you remember a little boy being killed by a train when we were growing up?"

"I remember exactly!" He's almost yelling. "I was there! My brother Jon, Pam Cowley, and I were riding our bikes, and we had just stopped to talk to this guy. I don't remember his name, and we didn't know him well. We were just kids on bikes riding downtown. After we rode away, I heard the train coming. Then the screech, and then an awful sound. We turned around and rode back. There was blood e-v-e-r-y-w-h-e-r-e. And body parts. I must have been eleven or twelve and it scared me. It changed me."

Is it wrong that his memory excites me? That I feel like I did when I uncovered forty boxes of old comic books at a junk store in Missoula, Montana once? That I have another in my series of "strange Bessemer deaths" to write about?

I begin obsessing about this story. I can't get back to Bessemer for another few weeks, but it hits me that someone has set up a "Fond Memories of Bessemer" page on Facebook. On November 12 at 11:20 a.m., I post a question about the death of Terry Wenndt. The first response comes in eleven minutes later. For the next three days, my phone app lights up regularly, chillingly, thrillingly. I learn so much about the accident, about old Bessemer friends, and people I might never have thought of again.

It's like coloring a blank page.

IV

I wonder if it's his name or the circumstances that stir so many people's memories of Terry Wenndt. One person remembers that her first grade class all walked together to the church for his funeral. Another person says her mother went to comfort Terry's mother, bringing food and warmth as people normally do in times of death.

What Cindey Huckabee remembers are the nightmares that followed her for weeks after seeing his casket.

A girl I knew back then, Allison McDonald Arnett, writes that when she saw my post, she quickly contacted her sister Lynn who told Allison that Terry "...was in her class the year it happened:

"We were in the grocery store with our mother [the A&P on Carolina Avenue], just across the street from the train tracks, when the train hit Terry. That's why it's so ingrained in my memory," Allison says. "I always thought, and Lynn confirmed, that he tried to beat the train, and his bike either got stuck on the tracks or he fell while crossing. Lynn thinks her teacher was in the store, too, when it happened. She also remembers going home and watching the news that evening, and that's when she learned who was in the accident."

Another old friend, Don Bowen, says that his father, a special agent in charge of investigating "wrecks, accidents, and thefts" for Southern Railroad, "worked the accident."

And Susie Seals, who was in my first grade class and with me off and on throughout high school, Googled the accident. The date, she says, was Saturday, April 8, 1967.

So finally I can place time. I can confirm my brother's memory. I was in the fifth grade during that spring, Mrs. Shivers' class. Allison's sister Lynn was a grade behind me, making both she and Terry Wenndt fourth graders, in either Miss Ball's or Mrs. Harwell's class.

At the tail end of the Fond Memories of Bessemer responses came one from another boy I knew back then, Yogi Padalino:

"I live in the house that Terry lived in back then. His brother stopped by a while back. He has two brothers—Randy and Timmy. The address is 1508 Dartmouth Avenue."

Five blocks from my family's house, but we didn't know them at all. So close, and yet, so far.

V

Memories fade, but return violently when enough people contribute to the remembering.

Thanksgiving weekend 1967, outside that same A&P on Carolina Avenue, just a few hundred yards from where Terry Wenndt was crushed on those train tracks, the janitor of our church, Buford White, is shot in the heart by a distraught white man whose wife left him that afternoon.

A month later, Christmastime, I receive my first ever bicycle, a red Skyrider. My parents forbid me to ride it in the street, however, which leaves me coasting down the sidewalk. The following summer, they relent, and I am free to travel anywhere, even over railroad tracks. I don't understand why they worry so much. I know the streets are dangerous, but all my friends ride them. I never come close to having an accident, and as I ride, it's like that boy and the train never collided, never even met. He fades away, and it's as likely as not then that he'll fade away for good. Forever.

And yet, here he is before me. What is the trigger? Is it that my thoughts have turned to death in my hometown? Or that I'm overseeing my college students drawing and coloring their own graphic novels, the memories of their lives? Or that I'm asking my creative nonfiction students to investigate a scene from their past and that their accounts are so deep and personal that I can't stand the beauty and the often horrifying tragedy?

Or is it that recently my wife and I have taken to biking on the Swamp Rabbit Trail in our current home in Greenville, SC, she on her brand new Schwinn 20-speed, I on my K-Mart tourist bike, as similar to the one I had in 5th grade as I can get? Red, with no gears.

At one point on the trail we have to negotiate train tracks. There's a sign posted nearby asking you to be cautious, or perhaps even to walk your bike across. In any case, you're supposed to cross the tracks perpendicularly to keep your tires from getting stuck. Once, we waited for ten minutes as a slow train approached. I'll admit that at first when I saw it coming, I was tempted to urge us to go faster, to race ahead and beat it. But there were others in front of us, adults and a few little boys and girls. We weren't in any hurry, had no place we'd rather be. So the saner part of me relaxed into the waiting, believing that time would pass as it's supposed to. That soon enough the other side would appear, and we'd be on our way to the end of the trail and the Leopard Forest Coffee Company. Wholly and happily.

It's a belief I would have liked Terry Wenndt to imagine.

And draw. A picturesque scene he could have colored of all the days he should have had.

9
How Could I Tell On Another?

She wasn't just seventeen. She was only ten, eleven at best. It's hard to tell now because back then she had already been left behind one grade that I know of: first grade, and I'm assuming it was just that one time.

Her name was Billie Bell. Stop for a second and try to picture a ten-year old girl named Billie Bell. What do you think she looks like? I'll start you out. Dirty blond hair in pixie-cut bangs. Skinny. What did Holden Caulfield call it? Roller-skate skinny? Oh yeah. She was poor, not the poorest in our class, but definitely challenged in holding clothes together enough to keep her warm in winter. Dresses that were never patched or worn through, but getting there. If she had a heavy coat, all I see now is something beige, maybe with a thin, fake-fur top. But mainly I remember her sweaters. Nothing bright, nothing pullover. Just those thin off-white ones that she never buttoned, although she always seemed cold to me. Her hygiene wasn't the worst either. Some of the more downtrodden grammar school kids smelled bad, and some showed visible dirt patches on their upper arms. Billie was never like this; I never smelled anything bad coming off of her, but that still didn't stop most of the boys from yelling "Cooties" if one of us ever, purely by accident, touched her.

I remember her for several reasons. One is that when she was determined—solving a math problem at the chalkboard, defying an attempt to be bounced out of a dodge ball game (she never succeeded but would always grin after being hit with that oversized red rubber ball)—her tongue would protrude from her mouth and she would bite down on it. Her way of showing how earnest she was; how great her effort was. When she did this, she looked like "Nanny," my maternal grandmother. So yes, even now when I see Billie Bell, I see my Nanny.

Another reason I remember her is her teeth, or rather, her upper gums. While her front teeth were mismatched and irregular (They weren't *so* bad and years later I saw the same teeth on my Rock and Roll idol Neil Young), Billie Bell would never wear braces. Her family would never be able to afford braces. Neither could mine for that matter.

But those gums. The way they looked *was* way beyond compare.

She didn't smile easily or often. Given her academic and social struggles, why should she? Given a home life that, admittedly, I knew nothing about, why would she? But when she did—perhaps after hearing the teacher say something warm; perhaps on seeing one of her few friends; perhaps when seeing that year's Christmas cookies displayed for all to enjoy—it was her gums that truly smiled.

Big red gums that overwhelmed those misshapen teeth.

Gums that I am afraid no young lover would ever want to make contact with.

As I said, Billie didn't smile that often. But her smile was eminently preferable to her cries.

I remember seeing her cry only once, but I remember it so vividly because, of course, I was the boy who made her cry.

On the occasions when our enormous, elderly, and deaf fourth-grade teacher, Miss Navie Ball, left the classroom—most likely to head to the cafeteria to supplement her mid-morning or early afternoon snack—she'd appoint one of us as class monitor, which was nothing but a sanctioned method of allowing kids to tell on each other. The monitor would compile a list of anything wrong or felonious that his or her classmates did, and in this process most of us learned, whether we understood it or not, what life in old Bavaria was like in the mid 1930's. Really, if you even whispered one syllable of a word loud enough and the monitor heard it, you went down on the list. And when Miss Ball returned and saw the list? Actually, I don't remember the exact penalty, though it was likely a journey to the principal's office or a note to your parents. Once, however, I did see her physically lift a boy named Don Franklin right off the ground and fling him across the room as if he were a paper Frisbee. What had been his offense? Simply being out of his seat, looking at what one of his friends had drawn. But, as you'll see, he deserved something of this sort for his future crimes.

We all wanted to be class monitors. For nothing seems more crucial to a fourth-grade child than being in charge, being able to give orders. Being the source of fear.

My turn came on a sunny day in late winter. Our classroom emitted steam heat so we were all comfortable, if not a bit glowing. I sat at Miss Ball's desk, my beady-blue eyes taking in all. The monitor doesn't have to let the offender know when he or she has transgressed, and so the power seems infinite and unchecked. Most monitors seek out those who have bothered, annoyed, or actually hurt them in previous months. Next, are the previous monitors who deserved their own date with the principal.

Much later, I saw what our monitors really were: Kapos. The most hated of the hated.

But back then, in my classroom monitoring time, I must have written down ten or eleven names in the seven minutes Miss Ball was away, devouring more corn muffins. And when she returned, she simply took my list and began calling out the names:

Brenda Gwin

Mike Folker

Keith Clark (one of my best friends)

Billie Bell.

What any of them had done, I knew even then, was nothing really. Passing a note; getting out of their seat; laughing at something foreign and unknown to me. Billie, I think, simply asked her tablemate a question. Softly, quietly, she disturbed nothing and no one. She never did.

I don't remember the other offenders' reactions now. Perhaps red faces or steely stares.

But I do remember Billie's.

She looked at me, and I, I could see.

And then she started crying, and as Mrs. Ball took her out of the room, I heard her. We all heard her:

"But what did I do? What did I do?"

I didn't know the word "inconsolable" then.

But right then when she crossed that room, my heart went boom. And so I re-entered the company of my peers, where I sat in a world of my own. In some ways, I think I'm still sitting there.

Still, that wasn't the worst thing I ever did to her. Thankfully, she never knew this other thing. This thing that I did that was so horribly normal and therefore, infinitely worse.

It was the Christmas party back in mid-December. Or rather, two weeks before the party when we all drew names for our "secret Santa." I originally drew "Samuel Ware," not one of my close friends, but a solid guy, unusual only in his Hawaiian background: dark, exotic, very Polynesian-looking. He was a safe "get," though, and I had a few minutes to ponder what I might buy him. Until:

"Hey Terry!"

It was Don Franklin, sidling up in a gesture of, I now see, desperation.

"I got Randy Ford's name, but I'm already buying him something because our families always swap gifts. So do you wanna switch with me?"

Randy was also a good friend of mine, and given the harmless nature of this request along with the benefit of bestowing my friend with a new game or Hot Wheels set of cars, I thought, why not?

"OK."

"Great. Here ya go," and he grabbed Samuel Ware right out of my hand and replaced it with...

Billie Bell.

Don squirmed his way back across the room, and I couldn't yell out, "Hey, you lied! You stuck me with Billie Bell!"

Thank God I didn't do that, though I know a few who might have.

But what I did do, naturally, was follow Don's model.

I don't think I have to explain why the thought of giving Billie Bell a Christmas present was so abhorrent to Don Franklin and to me. But I need to. It had something to do with our names forever being associated; with the rest of the class linking us; and with Billie somehow getting the impression that he, that I, actually didn't mind her.

That I liked her.

So I sought out three, four, five classmates, pulling Don's trick, until finally someone just as gullible as me responded and made the illicit trade. I got "Jennifer Jones," an athletic and tall girl who, as fate played it, got my name too. Whatever I gave her is lost to me. What she gave me was a Dr. Ben Casey jigsaw puzzle. My family and I spent that Christmas working on it, the green surgeon's scrubs on five different characters driving us all crazy. And when we got to the end, what drove us even crazier was that three or four pieces were missing.

Maybe it was Elise Harris, or Marie Ashley—a gorgeous, slim girl with long blond hair—whom I suckered in for Billie's name: a name virtually no one wanted to see, just as you never wanted to see the Old Maid card at the end of your fingers, drawn out of a full deck. But in the end, someone did get stuck with her name, and that someone, Elise or Marie, had to buy her a gift whether she wanted to or not.

But whatever it turned out to be—a pencil set, a pair of gloves—Billie accepted that present on the Christmas of her fourth-grade year, never knowing the truth of what went on behind her scenes. She ate the iced sugar cookies that Randy's mother brought and sang the Christmas carols with Miss Ball and the rest of her classmates, as if nothing were wrong. As if everything was beyond compare.

Which maybe it was at our fourth grade Christmas party at 2:00 on the last Friday before Christmas. After that day we had a two-week holiday, returning just after New Year's, most of us adorned in new clothes, comparing all our winter gifts.

And Billie looked the same of course, no worse for the wear really. Never knowing or suspecting or feeling jealous or hurt.

After grammar school, I lost touch with Billie. But in saying that, I realize that because of my own mechanisms, rising out of fear and insecurity and the need not to be ridiculed, I never really was in touch with her.

Or with myself back then.

I don't know what Billie has lived with for all the decades after grammar school, or how she's lived at all. But I do know how I've lived, and with what scenes, what memories. Memories of the way she looked and of how she might have danced if only the circumstances and the music had been right.

10
Dead Men Don't Drink Chlorine

It's an early summer day in 1965, at a swimming pool in Roosevelt Park, Bessemer, Alabama. I'm face down in the shallow water attempting to accomplish the dead man's float.

And failing.

The last day of third grade was just a weekend ago. The first day of swimming lessons is today. The next week will bring Vacation Bible School where I will build yet another bird feeder or shoeshine kit for Dad who is not even a member of this faith. Someone there will say something about the Jews, like always. I'll be embarrassed and pretend I don't exist, hoping no one catches on. But that's next week. This week, instead of playing like a dead man, I'm learning to float like one.

Most of my friends already know how to swim just like they've already been riding bikes for a few years now. I, however, can do neither. It will be two years before I even get my first bike, but in this pool, at this time, as I stand alongside a bunch of first and second graders waiting my turn to fail yet again at the most basic in-pool experience there is, I have nothing to show but last year's too tight bathing suit. I am taller by a foot than my fellow swimees, and weigh at least twenty pounds more than the kid next in size to me. Every one of them floats with ease, like ducks in a....

I hate them.

Fifty years later, I wonder if floating really can be taught. Isn't it innate in most of us? "You should have floated easy," my brother says when I tell him this story. "It's just natural."

My mother-in-law floats in the ocean. She can't swim, but she ventures out farther than anyone else in our family, flips on her back, and floats for hours, barely even fluttering her feet. No one else can sustain her level of floating, and most of us don't even try. Is she naturally buoyant? Or is she an anomaly? And if so, are there people the opposite of her, anomalies who most naturally sink?

Too bad this information about her can't reach the nine year-old me. The me who watches his swim class enviously. The me who now longs to build shoeshine kits. The me who sinks in water of any kind.

In the pool, attempting this rudimentary skill, I look like a tent, halfway raised. From the moment I start, my arms and legs, crab-like, begin clutching water on their way downward to the pool bottom. Gravity exists even in water, I am discovering, and its pull is stronger than my desire to float. There goes my waist, my stomach, my chest, and now I am standing upright again, facing my instructor, who is shouting at me:

"You're not floating! What's the matter with you? Can't you get it? Float like a dead man!!!"

His name is Jerry Lawley. And I guess he's seen dead men float before, but I haven't. Jerry attends Bessemer High School just down the street—a place where I will not follow him one day because in five more years the city fathers will build a new school in the western part of Bessemer in hopes of escaping integration. They won't succeed, at least not in the escape. I'll attend this high school along with 1700 other white and black kids, all of us crammed into a structure built for 800, while old Bessemer High will become a middle school and then the Kingdom Hall of

Jehovah's Witnesses. And that's how Bessemer achieves progress.

But neither Jerry nor I care about school or integration now. We are interested in progress, though, and so we both focus on Jerry who, once again, demonstrates the float. Next, he gets the youngest boy in class, a kindergartner named Matt, to demonstrate as well. Matt floats flawlessly.

"Your turn now," Jerry commands. And just as flawlessly, I sink.

"Maybe if you weren't so fat you could float," Jerry says.

Maybe, but I always thought it was the heavier object that was better suited to float.

"I've never seen anyone who couldn't float. Even my three year-old niece can float."

I'm glad his three-year-old niece isn't here, for I have no doubt that if she were, she'd be floating all around me, taunting me. Is floating tied to age; am I past my floating prime?

At the end of the first day's two-hour lesson, I've swallowed pool water, had its chlorine-saturated contents burn my eyes bright red, but I haven't floated, not even a little bit. When my mother arrives, she asks how I've done. She must figure that by now I've swum several lengths of the pool. Like most embarrassed children, I refuse to answer her except to say, "OK." If I told her I hated swimming, that I wanted to quit and never learn or get in any body of water short of the bathtub again, she'd get angry.

"But you have such a good time in the pool," she'd insist. "You know, swimming is so good for you. It's healthy and fun, and it's a skill you need. Besides, you want to be like the other kids, don't you?"

The other kids who float.

So since I can't speak my shame and have no other reason for not returning, there I am at Roosevelt Park the next afternoon, standing among my not-so-peers, facing the pool. And Jerry.

"Well, there's old Leadbelly again."

And we're off. Of course, I'm not off, and I'm definitely not floating. I'm in three feet of water, sinking faster than any material object that you can name. Jerry is teaching the other kids to add a kick to their float, and so all around me, the water is churning, and kids are popping up at breath's end, gasping but laughing. Jerry claps for them, puts Matt on his shoulders and swirls him around.

Me, he ignores.

Maybe if I could try kicking, I could propel myself beyond floating or the need to float. But no one explains to me this physical concept, and certainly no one gives me permission to try this law of motion. This act of life.

It's funny, but as I learn to ride a bicycle a couple of years later, neither will anyone explain to me how pedaling can help me stay upright and in motion. For two days I'll try to coast, feet dangling by the bicycle sides, the bike rolling a couple of feet at a time down our concrete sidewalk. I'll fall often, yet I'll climb back on every time. Finally, I'll unpurposely roll into some grass, and then weirdly, but instinctively, somehow my feet will reach for the pedals. After that, there's no stopping me; I'll ride everywhere, or at least the sidewalk in front of my house, with confidence and ease. What a difference self-propulsion makes.

But back in this pool I'm not encouraged or given permission to kick. For those two hours, and then for the remaining three days, Jerry says nothing more to me. It's hard to understand: in the weeks leading up to my first lesson, most of my friends told me the hardest thing I'd have to get used to was the sting of the chlorine. But at week's end, I'm still hovering in shallow water, unable to float or do much of anything really. Whatever my mother paid for these lessons is as drained as the pool will be in another year.

At Bible school the next week, our teacher describes that holy site, the Dead Sea, to us:

"It's so salty and dense, you can float on it without trying," Mr. Gibson assures us.

I wonder, though, and mostly what I wonder is not whether I could float there, but whether I'd be willing to cast myself off in a place where the water itself is pronounced dead.

It's early August. We've just returned from a family vacation to St. Petersburg Beach where I waded in the shallow ocean water every day without ever going under or needing to float. Now, my mother says it's time to return to the pool, to continue my swimming lessons. I didn't know this was coming.

I'm still in the beginning class, but the swimmers are all new; no one from my previous failure is there to see me or to know.

Not even Jerry Lawley.

Instead there are two teenaged girls waiting for us.

"Hi, I'm Leslie, and this is Jill. We're cousins, and we're going to help you guys learn how to swim."

They're so pretty. Leslie is blond and says she's fifteen. Jill is darker and fourteen. They're nice, but more than anything else, they're patient.

"We know you guys can learn," Leslie says. "It isn't always easy, but don't worry. If you have trouble, that's OK. You know, when I first learned to swim, I had the hardest time staying afloat."

To be honest, she didn't really say that last part. But I did see it in her eyes. And another thing that helps: Before we get in the pool, I look up and see my friend Paul heading our way.

"Can you swim already," he asks. "I can't."

"I can't either," I say.

Today I know that what happened to me then was a release of pressure in an environment conducive to learning and feeling safe. At that time, though, all I knew was that I wasn't alone.

Leslie and Jill work with groups of four. They take us out one at a time, helping us to feel what floating is like. They don't mention "dead men" or failure, or who is and isn't fat.

I feel Leslie holding my stomach and back as I drift in the water. It feels good, but I'm also worrying that when she lets go, so will I. She talks through my worries, though, encouraging me, praising me—as if I'm really accomplishing a great feat—and as I wonder when she'll let go, I hear her say:

"Look at you! You're doing it. You're floating by yourself."

I open my eyes in the pool, and what I see is the pool bottom. What I don't see are my legs or feet or stomach. I float on for at least another ten seconds, and when I come up for air, Leslie says:

"That's great Buddy! You floated for almost 30 seconds. Keep trying and see how long you can go."

The rest of the afternoon I'm dead in the water—as dead as Paul and all the other kids. The next day I add a kick, and by week's end I'm stroking quickly and steadily, still with my head in the water, mindless of the depth and the chlorine.

The following week, Jill teaches me rhythmic breathing. I have trouble here, but not because of her. My trouble is the deep water. Turning my head for air, stroking in time, and wondering whether I can still touch bottom make me lose my concentration. So instead I hold my breath and swim straight on with my face in the water for as long as I can go—hopefully, to the other pool edge. Sometimes I don't make it, and when I stop, I take a big gulp of air and keep going. I feel ashamed that I can't breathe in rhythm and hope no one notices.

Yet, what I notice now as I see this scene, is a boy who didn't give up, who kept going in an act of will and strength.

A boy who refused to sink.

And though I never did get rhythmic breathing down, I learned enough in those two weeks to last me, to allow me to proclaim to everyone "I can swim." To keep me returning to any form of water as often as I could.

Which, as far as the pool at Roosevelt Park went, was never again.

I told you at the beginning that this was Alabama in 1965, the year that schools in my district finally integrated. The process was slow but never steady. Never in rhythm, never even treading water. I know that in some districts, people advocated closing the schools down. They didn't do that in Bessemer, but before the season started the following summer, they did close our only public pool. Sitting next to a Black child was one thing. Getting the water where they had just swum in your white eyes was another.

Dead Men Don't Drink Chlorine / 121

So the city fathers poured rich red Alabama clay into the pool where I learned to float.

Today, that space has been incorporated into a baseball field, which will soon be cemented over to make way for a senior activities center. I'm very hopeful that somewhere on these grounds they'll also build a nice, chlorinated pool for those elderly black and white swimmers and for all those others who, in the time they have left, choose only to float.

11
The Mayor

I'm sitting in my mother's den watching my daughters take turns brushing "Pepper," my mother's Maine Coon. Mom is watching "Dateline," another grisly episode about a husband murdering his wife. Two former Baptist missionaries, the voiceover tells us.

"Hhhmph," Mom says. "Baptist missionaries my foot!"

I love her righteous indignation, maybe because it's her most familiar default, reminding me of front porch chats or her end of neighborly phone calls.

The "Dateline" narrative continues, and I turn back to reading Alabama football message boards. We're in town for tomorrow's game, Alabama versus Southern Mississippi. Not a great matchup, but all I could manage given costs and my daughters' availability from work and school.

As I read about the ongoing quarterback controversy—an old story between champions of either the Black or a white quarterback—I realize that my mother is in mid-sentence, addressing me:

"...that time when Frank Sinatra, Jr sang at the Knights of Columbus Hall in Bessemer?"

"When I was in high school? Yeah, I remember. I double-dated that night with Jimmy Walker. Sarah Monte asked him to go, and Pat Pace asked me. I'll never forget it. Pat's father was a detective on the Bessemer force. When he opened the door and got a look at me with my long red hair, I felt like I was ready for a police lineup. He never said a word to me, and that was the only date I had with Pat Pace."

"OK, but do you remember what a fool Jess Lanier made of himself that night?"

Jess Lanier was Bessemer's longtime mayor. I'm guessing that the year of that show was 1973, so by then Lanier had been mayor for at least twelve years, which would seem to confirm a status of "beloved," for His Honor. I remember having my picture made with him in his office when I was a Cub Scout. He was officially recognizing Scout Week, and there were two older scouts in the office too. In the photograph, the Mayor leans over his desk from his leather-backed swivel chair to sign the official proclamation. He looks up at the camera as he signs, and smiles. Flanking him, the three of us smile, too, like I'm sure we've been asked to. I have no more idea now why I was selected for this honor than I did then.

I think now that it's too bad Pat Pace's father hadn't seen that picture—me in uniform with the Mayor and with my very buzzed crew cut. But given all that would happen that night, leaving the Mayor out of our hostile meeting was best.

Mayor Lanier's voice had that medium-hoarse Southern quality endemic to those who considered themselves true gentlemen. He tried to put us at ease with small talk. I kept thinking, "Here I am in a mayor's office. I wonder what happens here?" I had seen the mayor before at our church, First Methodist. He came irregularly but always made a grand entrance a minute or two before services started. His daughter, Gingah, had been my Bible School teacher the previous summer. She was also head majorette at Bessemer High. Imagine.

Our photo appeared in the following week's *Bessemer Cutoff News*, a weekly Thursday insert in *The Birmingham News*. My mother taped it into my baby book. I think it's still there. My smile is the usual one: all lips and no teeth. But what strikes me the most is that the Mayor's pose is identical to the ones of him published every week signing yet another proclamation favoring our town. If I hadn't been in his presence, I'd think he was a life-sized cutout, trying to prove that he did *something* while serving our city.

And he did do some things. Jess Lanier mayored our town from the late 50's through the mid-70's which means he "led us" through the integration of our public spaces. I have no inside information of his Honor's intentions, but here are a few things I do know about "his" Bessemer:

Our cafes had separate rear entrances, or carry out windows, for "colored people," at least until 1966. Our five-and-dime stores had separate lunch counters, drinking fountains, and one unisex restroom marked "colored." I tried drinking from that colored-marked fountain in Pizitz Department store when I was a boy of three. The family who escorted me to downtown that day promptly escorted me away from the fountain and suggested I begin learning how to spell, starting with the words "white" and "colored."

I see this moment so clearly even after fifty-five years as I'm standing with my wife and mother in the old Pizitz building, now a United Fabric store, looking for material for our new curtains. I show my wife the spot on either side of the second floor elevator where those water fountains were. You can't tell now that they were ever there, and I can't decide if that's a good thing or some-thing very bad.

It's on this same floor that my mother bought my Cub Scout uniform, the one I wore in the picture with the Mayor. I remem-ber watching the clerk select my golden kerchief and the rounded metal clap that bound it about my neck. That day my mother also bought me an official Cub Scout knife—though I couldn't "play" with it, she said—and the certified Cub Scout Handbook. I remember learning the Cub Scout pledge that very night:

"On My Honor, I will do my best to do my duty to be square, and to obey the laws of the pack."

Vague words, unknown laws. More than anything now, I can see the glass counter where the clerk stacked my new supplies. And my mother, our new "Den Mother," proudly paying for them all.

Our Mayor also oversaw the closing of Roosevelt Park's public swimming pool in 1966, the only public pool in the city, where I had learned to swim the previous summer. The city fathers filled it with red dirt and then paved it smoothly with concrete. I guess they were serious about white and Black kids staying out of each other's water.

And of course Mayor Lanier regulated public school integration, which began in 1966, too. That was quite a year for Bessemer, and I know you can do the math, but anyway, our school system integrated itself twelve years after Brown versus Board of Education. So, born in 1956, by all rights I should never have spent any time in a segregated system. Of course, only certain citizens' rights were ever at issue.

It's unfair to charge Lanier with being solely responsible for these officially-sanctioned events, but after all, he was the Mayor. He wanted to be the Mayor, and he kept getting re-elected just as his compatriot George Wallace kept being returned to the Montgomery Governor's mansion (or if not Wallace, then his wife).

"I'm a Wallace man," Lanier once said, or could have.

In fact, Jess Lanier was a Wallace delegate at the 1972 Democratic National Convention in Miami, at which Democrats embraced a new age of politics and causes. On the platform during one of those prime-time convention nights stood an openly Gay man advocating Gay Liberation. I was on the verge of entering my junior year in high school that summer, and I'll never forget that the week after the convention, one of my best friends, who would come out a few years later, called me:

"You won't believe it. Jess Lanier was quoted in *Time Magazine*. He's angry because they've let queers speak at the convention. Isn't that so typical of Bessemer?"

You can read the mayor's words on your own if you have

access to the July 24, 1972, issue of *Time* (p. 24). If you don't:

"There on the podium at the convention was a certified member of Gay Liberation nonchalantly addressing the party...'Goddam,' said Jess Lanier, mayor of Bessemer, Alabama. If that's what they're going to talk about, we're never going to get this party together again. They haven't got a dog's chance of electing a President on this platform. Damn, do they need Wallace!" ("Dissidents: The Wallace Factor")

The literary analyst in me wants to go through every word of that quotation dissecting and deconstructing and reminding the readers of all the ironic nuances. But I'll just leave it at the weirdly prophetic voice of the Mayor understanding that the Democrats had no chance in '72, not with that platform, not with McGovern, and certainly not against the sitting President.

I think now about Lanier's image, the one he photographed to the rest of the country in that story. I think about his blustering on the convention floor, the behavior of an old-fashioned Southern demagogue. Of an old-fashioned Southern boor.

Of a man who, on the night of the Frank Sinatra Jr, show, demonstrated all that he was.

"Don't you remember what a fool Jess Lanier made of himself that night," my mother continues. "When he got so drunk and insisted on making a speech at the intermission?"

I remember the Knights of Columbus Hall, a nondescript white building on Bessemer's lower, northern end. I can still see the four or five long tables decorated in white cloth and fresh spring flowers; my parents sitting somewhere behind me, and Jackie and Paula Lampkin sitting right across from me. Jackie and Paula are a mother-daughter team who deserve their own story one day, but on this night, for some reason, I ask Paula if I can have a sip of her water. Jackie—the archetype of all future Helicopter or Tiger Moms—shouts and grabs the glass away:

"You're not going to drink after Buddy Barr and get *his* germs!"

I have no idea why I didn't ask my own date for water. Maybe I was still thinking about her father, a lieutenant in Jess Lanier's force.

Despite all this, I remember listening to Sinatra Jr sing his father's hits. He looked like his father and sounded like him too, for whatever that's worth. I remember "Come Fly With Me," and that when he veered into "Strangers in the Night," at least one Italian mother swooned. Truthfully, his singing was pleasant enough even for a kid like me who preferred Santana or Neil Young. At least the dulcet refrains filled the more-than-awkward silence between Pat and me.

To be fair, Pat looked very pretty that night, wavy hair flowing down her back, proudly displaying the wrist corsage I gave her. I'll never know why she asked me to this show. Back then, I never believed a girl could have a crush on me. I'm tempted now to look her up on Facebook and message her to see if she remembers that night: the Lampkins and Frank Jr.

And Jess Lanier who, according to my mother, drunkenly slurred the same stories over and over as he tried to welcome our visiting "star" to Bessemer, the "Marvel City," at a club where Lanier wasn't even a member, but at an event he figured deserved his official imprimatur.

At this point, though, I have to add the one other change in Bessemer that transpired, or was instigated under Jess Lanier's watch.

As a boy I dreamed of attending Bessemer High, a three-story, reddish-brown brick structure that commanded an entire city block, just three streets west of the center of downtown. I could see myself standing on its grounds after school, strolling one block over to The Spinning Wheel for a milkshake with my friends before either walking or driving the nine blocks home. And in those dream-years, I never doubted that this would be my course.

But in those dreams I also never counted on the 60's, the convulsions of integration, and all that our city fathers would perform or enact to keep the affluent white kids in a school of their own. So when the courts ordered desegregation, and when it became apparent to everyone that Bessemer High was destined for a zone that would draw a healthy percentage of "colored" kids, our city fathers built a new school in the trendier and wealthier western part of town. A lead-colored brick edifice in the shape of a tic-tac-toe grid, this new school boasted no windows. The architects and even the tenants, however, thought that the state-of-the-art sunken gymnasium more than made up for the darkness. Designed for only 800 students—there were exactly 800 lockers—in a city that on any given year contributed at least 3000 high school age kids, the plan would have been foolproof had the courts looked the other way, had they consented to another year of separation without representation.

Had Bessemer been allowed to keep three ongoing public high schools: one all-Black (Abrams High on the east side), one all-white (the new school on the west side), and the other somewhere in-between (Bessemer High).

The new school, someone decided, should be named for the Mayor, thus: Jess Lanier High found itself birthed. It's the school Sarah Monte, Jimmy Walker, Pat Pace, and I attended for our entire high school life, along with 1700 other kids each year. For in the end, not even the eponymous Mayor could circumvent the courts or the reality of full integration. Old Bessemer High became a middle school and eventually the Kingdom Hall of Jehovah's Witnesses.

And while I never strode its grounds as a student, I did, as a member of the Thespian club, perform on its stage in my sophomore year play, *Harvey*. For among other forgotten features, Jess Lanier High had no auditorium.

Still, at Jess Lanier High we students were always close. We shared lockers, rotating lunch periods, over-flowing classes and classrooms. We had an integrated student body, a football team with a star white quarterback and a star Black receiver who, back at Abrams High, had been the star quarterback. We had integrated faculty, coaches—all having been collapsed from the former segregated schools. We even had an integrated smoking section outside of the band room.

Clearly, we had it all.

Or at least some of us did. I doubt that the kids who rode the buses to school from as far as seven miles away thought so. They often got to school by 6:45 and then waited for their day to begin in that sunken gym where, I'm told, the heat never flourished in winter. Often, these same kids wouldn't reach home until 5 or 5:30, even though the last bell rang at 3:00.

People much younger than me ask now what school was like in those troubling days—how I handled the problems and tensions of race. I tell them that as a student who got dropped off at 7:50 by his parents every morning and whose ride was waiting at 3 every afternoon, I was always mindful of my privileges even when I was intimidated by the words, the anger, and sometimes the actual fights around me. Because with so much closeness, there were always people getting in your way, making you feel crowded and even disrespected. Making you lose your cool and act badly.

Which brings me back to the end of my mother's story.

"That's right. That Jess Lanier was making such a spectacle of himself that finally Margaret Bivona came up to the stage and told him off. She told him that he was embarrassing himself and everyone else, and that he should get off the stage and go home. She probably shouldn't have done it, but he was being such a fool. And the next thing you know, he was rearing back and acting like he was going to hit her."

"Oh my God," I said, and I wasn't sure if the image was really coming back to me or if my mother's description was so precise that I couldn't help but see our Mayor looming over this little Italian woman.

"Yessir. Pig House and Tommy Norton had to hold him back. If they hadn't, I believe he would have sure nuff hit her!"

Our Mayor, Jess Lanier, come to life. I wonder now, given the context, if he was merely doing things "his way" like he always had?

But finally the Mayor was pacified, and Frank Jr. finished the show. Jimmy and I drove our dates home. I walked Pat to her door where her daddy was waiting. We were all very proper, very self-aware. But then, the only spotlight on us was our own.

I don't remember now the year Jess Lanier died. His wife followed him some years later, and just this past year, his daughter Gingah died of some form of cancer. The KC Hall where Jess Lanier almost hit Margaret Bivona, and Jackie Lampkin said my germs weren't good enough for her daughter Paula, and the son of America's greatest singer entertained 100 or so people on a brisk Bessemer Thursday night, fell into ruination a couple of decades ago. It's been relocated near the rebuilt Catholic church close to Bessemer's Super Wal-Mart, which itself is very near the new Bessemer City High School, an institution that is predominantly populated by African-American students. Jess Lanier High is now Bessemer City Middle School. I don't know, because a gate now guards its entrance, but I guess it still has that sunken gym and no windows. However, both schools currently share the legendary nickname of old Bessemer High, a nickname dating back some eighty-plus years: the Purple Tigers.

For after all, some things need to stay the same so that we'll remember, and maybe so that other people, younger than ourselves, will ask uncomfortable questions about echoing things they don't quite, but feel they should, understand. About why things *are*, and for too many people, why they could never be.

12
Classified Secrets

Over our Thanksgiving meal, 2014, my mother revealed this secret:

"Dissie once told me that Mr. Mitchum next door tried to get all the maids who worked for him into bed."

It wasn't the texture of the turkey, of course, that caused my gagging. My daughters didn't know Mr. Mitchum; neither did my wife. Come to think of it, I didn't either. But we all went wide-eyed anyway.

"Grandma!" My daughters grew very attentive. "What happened?"

"That's what Dissie said. She said Tommie Lee told her to watch out for the old man."

"He didn't try that with Dissie did he Mom," I asked. The Mitchums and our family both employed Dissie, and I loved her as well as I did my own parents. After all, she raised me too.

"No, he died soon after Dissie came to work for us. But Dissie believed Tommie Lee. And I've never told that story till now."

I grew up in the most uncertain time of the Civil Rights era. So I knew that white people then were capable of anything—especially when that anything came to Black people. Back in the 50's, the Klan had a welcome sign on the outskirts of the city, next to the one erected by the Civitans Club. Things have changed a bit though. Today, as you get deeper into Alabama, along with the random raised Confederate battle flags, you see signs that say "Anti-Racism = Codeword for Anti-White."

And so even with this information, knowing all that I know, I am completely shocked to discover that the white man next door who died before I was born tried to bed his decidedly African-American maids. Am I really that naïve?

When my mother revealed this secret, I wanted to yell, "Is nothing sacred?" But I know that answer, too.

Sacred is as sacred does.

My brother Mike and I both had our battles with Mrs. Mitchum. I never knew her given name, oddly, as everyone called her "Willie," a nickname for what? Wilhemina? Willetta? She named her only son "William" and called him "Will." It seemed funny back then, but less so today given this late revelation about Willie's husband whom everyone called "Mitch." Mitch was an executive with the local foundry, and carrying on his corporate legacy, Willie subscribed to both *The Wall Street Journal* and *Barron's*—papers that seemed to me as somber and gray as Willie herself. On the days Dissie worked for her, I'd go visit her as she ironed or cleaned the kitchen. We'd listen to radio station WVOK and Dissie's favorite on-air personality, Joe Rumore, who called everybody "neighbor" and played all genres of music in those years. Our favorite song was Jimmy Dean's "Big Bad John," with which Dissie and I would sing along when Willie wasn't around.

Of course, when she was around, I wasn't allowed to visit.

Today, I remember "Mitch" only by the portrait of him hanging on the living room wall, just above the mantle. He seemed refined, stately in his brown suit, vest, and businessman's tie, and though he was half-smiling in the portrait, I got the distinct impression that he was anything but friendly and warm. Except, of course, when he was hunting down the Black women who worked for him.

I can't help picturing these images: Mitch chasing middle-aged, uniformed women through the swinging kitchen door and into the hall leading to the master bedroom. The master bedroom where once my mother attended to Willie when she was suffering from cataracts. The room where photos of Will in military dress hung on all four walls. He graduated from Virginia Military and though he gave me my first Frisbee and my first copy of *To Kill A Mockingbird*, both used, I remember him best in his photos: his cadet hat; the stare of steel that all cadets must wear.

I wonder how he must have looked to, and at, his father.

I guess I'm saying that back then, though they lived right next door to us in a house not very different and certainly not much bigger than ours, the Mitchums gave off a bearing of class bordering on regal importance—a bearing that distanced them from everyone else on the street.

And I guess I'm saying that while I knew that they were difficult and snooty, I never thought about what lay beneath their exterior. What they tried to get by with, or hide.

I guess I'm saying that I never examined those pictures as closely as I should have. Or maybe it's just that I didn't really know what I was seeing.

What I do know is that despite my small-town Alabama upbringing, because of The Beatles and rock and roll in general, I pushed my parents hard to let me grow my hair out of the crew cuts and flat tops and the neatly parted-on-the-side "good little boy" looks favored by small town life. From fifth grade on, I had Beatle-bangs, though until eighth grade, the backside of my head was still nearly shaved. By tenth grade, thanks to a relaxed high school dress code—too many other issues with race and over-crowding to worry about jeaned-clad girls and long-haired guys—my strawberry hair hit my shoulders. I felt liberated from my past and even admired by those very difficult and skittish high school girls. In ninth grade, I had been dismissed from school twice for having hair that covered my ear-tops; now I was in the top-five longest male-hair cuts of my entire school.

My parents griped and fussed about my appearance, yet during my struggles with the school dress code, they backed me all the way. My hair, it seemed, had finally become my own.

Occasionally a redneck would call me a sissy or whistle, but I didn't care. Or at least, I didn't show it.

It was harder, however, to face older adults who looked at me like I was some sort of Commie. And for some, like Willie, I guess I was.

She took it upon herself, every chance she got, to remark on my "long and ugly hair," how I didn't look "manly" like her Will had when he was my age. I did my best to be polite and say nothing but "Yes, ma'am." But once, after she felt particularly entitled to tell me about my obnoxious hair in the presence of my father, he let her have it:

"It's his hair and he can wear it any way he pleases. And you can mind your own damn business!"

Wow. My Dad, the World War Two infantry vet. His curly, almost kinky hair never touched his ears, collar, or fell forward at all. Though by 1973, he did sport long and bushy sideburns.

His rebuke stopped Willie cold, and she licked her particular wound for a few months until she saw another chance. Or rather, my teenage friends and I presented her with a golden wand.

Our youth group at First Methodist Church had been in-quiring about the possibility of conducting an entire morning's worship ourselves, and in the spring of 1972 we got our chance. One of us directed the choir, another led the Affirmation of Faith and Apostle's Creed, and my best friend Jimbo actually delivered the sermon. Sadly, my family was out of town on the big day, but before I left, I did get to participate in painting six-foot banners with youthful platitudes written on them to hang from the rafters of our sanctuary. I no longer remember what they said—that is, except the one that boldly and largely proclaimed,

"Jesus Had Long Hair Too!"

Which, according to all the paintings in our Sunday School classes, he did.

At some point during the following week, Willie saw me outside in my front yard and started yelling about our lack of reverence and respect—that we had sung songs from *Jesus Christ Superstar* and wore jeans and crocheted tunic-smocks for the service. She then crescendoed into her final and favorite point of offense:

"And just how do you know Jesus wore long hair?"

Her cataract-scarred eyes, behind coke-bottle glasses, glared at me.

I thought then, and more particularly again after this past Thanksgiving: "How do know he had pale skin?" I wish I had said it. I wish I had said that Jesus would have detested *The Wall Street Journal* and all it stands for. I wish I had said "Workers of the World Unite, you having nothing to lose but your long hair!" I wish I had said even a simple and plain "Right On!"

Back in those days, when our family and Willie shared Dissie's services, there was no minimum wage for maids, that is, if you paid them cash. We did at least pay for Dissie's social security and health care, but her weekly wage was embarrassing. I know we supported her through her nephew Billy's stint in Viet Nam and through presents to her and her family. I know that Dissie loved us and that like us, she had a difficult time dealing with Willie, who refused to increase Dissie's wage, ever, and never made her feel like she was a human being, certainly not during the fight for civil rights and definitely not while her nephew was serving his country in that misbegotten war. For there's this story, which occurred while Billy was away:

A neighbor on the other side of the alley discarded used linoleum flooring, piles of worn out tile. Willie, in a fit of self-sanctioned charity, decided that Dissie could use the tile, would *like* the tile, and so she hauled a few pieces into the house to "give" to her. But Dissie declined the offer, and after she reported the event the next day to my mother, old Willie promptly declared that Dissie was "an ungrateful Communist."

"Dissie doesn't even know what a Communist is," my mother told us later during supper. Still maybe some old linoleum was a better offer than Tommie Lee got from old Mitch.

Willie wasn't all bad. There was the time she cooked dinner for my brother and me when my mother was in the hospital undergoing a hysterectomy. My brother, though, remembers the dinner as some strange spaghetti concoction, which, along with meat and noodles, included walnuts and apples. Still, it was the neighborly thing.

And then there was the time Willie hired me to cut her grass after her regular "yard-boy," a young African-American guy named John, either quit on her or was fired. My mother warned me before I accepted the job:

"You know who you'll be working for!"

I thought I did, and after all, I had been cutting grass in the neighborhood for three years. I was thirteen then and just couldn't see how cutting one old woman's front yard could be troublesome.

After several cuts, Willie seemed pleased enough to give me another job. She took me down to the side of her house and showed me all the ivy that had overgrown her walkway up from her garage.

"Now, I don't want you to pull all of it; just make sure it's away from those steps."

Taking her at her word, I spent a couple of hours pulling ivy with my bare hands and clearing what I thought was sufficient room for any older person to maneuver without fear of tripping. When I knocked on her door to show her the results, she followed me down, stood very still as she surveyed my work through her bottle glasses, and pronounced rather shrilly,

"Why son, I don't see where you've pulled any ivy at all! I want this taken up!"

She continued staring at me for another minute, then turned and went on back to the house. It was too late that afternoon to finish, so the next morning, before I had any breakfast, I went back to the ivy patch and worked all morning pulling up the clinging vines. The neighbor on the other side of Willie, Mrs. Manzella, called out to me after I had been working an hour or so,

"Honey, have you had any breakfast?"

So hungry then that I couldn't lie, I gratefully accepted the plate of eggs, bacon, and toast she prepared. After only a ten-minute break, I went back to pulling and kept at it till noon.

Admittedly, I didn't pull every last strand of ivy, but she said she wanted some left. So again when I finished, I knocked on Willie's door to ask if she wanted to come see.

"No, I'm sure it's fine, son."

And then she gave me the three dollars she promised, enough money for me to buy the new Hot Wheels set I had been coveting.

That afternoon, my mother drove me downtown to buy my prize. I was so happy. I had worked hard and earned my money. As our car pulled back up in front of the house, though, what greeted me next door at Willie's house was this:

John, the former yard boy, cutting Willie's grass again.

I stood there holding my Hot Wheels set as Willie emerged to yell at me: "You still didn't get up all that ivy."

Though I felt the shame of such a public humiliation, my Hot Wheels set ran as smoothly as I dreamed it would anyway. And clearly, Willie thought that what went on outside of her house was worth all of her attention.

As a kid in Alabama during these times, things ran as smoothly as they could for me, given that the city fathers cemented over the community swimming pool, closed down Kiddie-Land, the only amusement park within 100 miles, and built new schools in outlying locales to avoid as best they could the infiltration and dilution of their race. During these times whole families, indeed whole neighborhoods, moved out of their ancestral homes rather than live next to, depending upon your social class, Negroes, Jigaboos, Coloreds, Darkies, Nigras, and of course, Niggers.

So, knowing all of this, I've been trying to understand my own shock at my mother's story—why it hit me so hard. Was it that I was simply stunned that I was so stunned? Was it that I thought despite everything—the racism, the fear, the hatred—our neighborhood was composed, at worst, *only* of people who were afraid of change, afraid of racial mixing? That at they very least, taking race out of the equation, in their personal relations with family, friends, and employees, the people in my neighborhood community were dignified—that they showed that dignity in most facets of life?

I don't know how ol' Mitch did it. How he got around his wife Willie; how he kept the maids from talking. Did he pay them extra? Did he hold their livelihood hostage? Did he threaten their families? How many maids were there?

I don't know if Willie ever knew. Maybe she did and the knowing caused her to inoculate herself against it with an extra layer of pride. In any case, she still kept that portrait of him prominently displayed till the end of her life.

I do know now that Tommie Lee told Dissie who, because she loved and trusted a younger white woman, told my mother. Trusted my mother. Dissie's been dead now for nearly twenty years, and old Willie for even longer.

Until last week, my mother never betrayed Dissie's trust. That's the dignity of friendship, of those who love and respect each other.

After the story at Thanksgiving, the writer in me had to ask if there were other tales like this one, buried in my mother's subconscious past. But she just shook her head:

"I know lots of stories," and then she got up from the table and headed toward the dishwasher. But just as swiftly, she returned.

"I'll tell you one more. When Willie was packing up her house before moving to the retirement village, she gave me a beautiful silver cruet that she knew I loved. I couldn't believe how generous she was being, but she said she wanted me to have it. I put it in the dining room hutch with my other fine pieces, and for six months, I looked at it and still couldn't get over her generosity. And six months to the day, she called me up and asked me to give it back. Said she found out how much it was worth and wanted to give it to her granddaughter. So I said, 'I'll put it out by the front door, and you can come get it whenever you want!'"

"Wow," my daughters exclaimed. "How much was it worth, Granma?"

"$75.00. Now what do you think of that?"

But no one said a word. And then we cleaned our plates, trying to digest all we had heard and all we'd never understand about the rituals, mindset, and misguided sense of propriety of a not-too-distant time in the places of our South.

13
But Pat Boone Never
Lived in Bessemer

On the night before I entered 7th grade, my across-the-street, 9th grade neighbor Joe, while we were enjoying spareribs at our family's annual Labor Day picnic, gave me this advice:

"Be careful tomorrow. You never know who's carrying a switchblade."

I grew up in the *switchblade* era. I'd hear talk at home about beer brawls in the rougher sections of town where combatants would pull switch-blade knives on each other and fight it out, often to the death. In fact, Joe's family's handy-man—Elijah who had conked red hair and carried his own ladder—was murdered in a switchblade fight. I knew Elijah. He was friendly enough, but my senses—or was it my grandmother's voice—warned me to not hang around him too long, as I did with the various other maids and yard men of our circle of friends. I was only ten when reports of the incident made their way through our neighborhood hotlines, the usual afternoon phone sessions where my mother and grandmother and all their friends might tie up the lines for literally hours.

"What does a switchblade look like," I asked Joe. At that

moment, I felt as threatened by a switchblade as I was by the cottonmouths that my parents told me slithered in and near the creek down the street from my house.

"Never mind what they look like," Joe cautioned. "Just keep close to the lockers and never get in the way of a ninth-grader, or anyone else for that matter. You never know who's been left-behind."

I couldn't enjoy the rest of my supper that night and refused the homemade vanilla ice cream altogether.

"It's OK," my Daddy said later. "Joe's Mom forgot to put sugar in it again."

So there I stood: My first day at Bessemer Jr. High in these switchblade times. The front entrance doors opened garage-door wide and I thronged in with my new classmates. The main office lurked just to the right of this entrance, which didn't really assure me that any "hood" wouldn't try to sneak in a dangerous weapon. Because, I noticed in my first breathtaking moment of junior high, the office had no windows on the door or elsewhere. And neither on this day or any other in my experience there did the principal—Mr. Camp, whose larynx had been crushed, reportedly, in some foreign war—nor the assistant principal—Mr. Davidson, a red-haired and, I'd been warned, hot-headed man—ever stand in the front doorway to frisk the entrants. Joe told me that if you ever got caught with a switchblade, you were automatically expelled. I wondered how, if they weren't checking at the door, our school guardians could ever catch anyone with that venomous weapon. I considered my chances of surviving that year fifty-fifty at best.

I hadn't been in school for a week when I saw my first fight, the first in what seemed an every-other-day occurrence. Once, Russell Aldrich tore a hunk of Don Griffis's hair out of the side of his head. Having a bald spot in seventh grade is maybe a badge of honor. It certainly didn't hurt Don's success with the girls. And then, a giant of a ninth grader, Biff Wyatt, allowed himself to be pummeled into submission by a wiry kid named Bobby Ray

Ledbetter. I saw Biff on the ground, struggling to cast off Bobby Ray's "bulk," his face a red ribbon of strain and shame. Most of these fights were set up during school hours and then enacted just after the 3:00 bell, behind the school and just beneath the gymnasium window. On any given week there might be a feature event three or four days straight; never was there a week with fewer than two.

Maybe the strangest and scariest of these for me occurred on a cold, cloudy afternoon in early December when, as I was walking up the hill to my Mom's car, I saw Bruce Duncan, the first Black kid I knew in elementary school, walking among a crowd of white boys. When I reached our car, they passed me, heading across the street and under the railroad viaduct. A few minutes later, our car passed, and in a vacant lot I saw Bruce, entangled on the ground with one of the boys. The others were gathered in a semi-circle watching, cheering, or so it seemed to me since our windows were rolled up as we passed. We turned the next corner, out of sight, but I kept thinking of that scene and how as they passed me on their way to the battle, they seemed like they were going over to someone's house for a game of football in the front yard.

I didn't see anyone with a switchblade during that grappling moment. Nor did I see one over the next few months of school, though like those snakes that I never saw either, I just knew that someone's switchblade was out there, somewhere, waiting for me.

Education is a funny experience. Not everything you see will educate you in the way that your guiding elders intend, and just when you're distracted enough from real or unreal fears, someone arises to impart a valuable lesson. Such was the case with my educational experience in the face of Pat Boone's immortal art film, *The Cross and the Switchblade.*

In my 7th grade year, I came home straight from school every day, and after a light snack, immediately tackled my homework. I was allowed to pause for a game of football with friends in my own front yard, but I could not watch TV until every last bit of my geometry, composition, or science homework lay exhausted in my notebooks. In my leisure time I read biographies of famous Americans; Ray Bradbury stories; Batman comics; and the Sports Page of *The Birmingham News*, our afternoon paper. While I didn't always eat my vegetables at dinner (steamed cauliflower smells exactly like sewage), I generally obeyed my parents' every command: I always asked permission to go to a friend's house; took out the garbage after supper; raked every leaf I could see in early fall. I was no cause for worry or alarm.

And I didn't need help from a born-again Christian crooner-turned-auteur.

Yet, as part of a Methodist Youth Fellowship experience, one winter Friday night, my church friends and I packed into Birmingham's Empire Theater to take in Pat Boone's personal epic. Munching my highly-salted popcorn, over the next ninety-five minutes I watched Pat take on and convert a switchblade-wielding gang. For all of those minutes, as I observed his white bucks, his plastic bromides, and his strangely combed hair, I just knew that he would be sliced to ribbons, packaged up, and delivered to the nearest 4-H clubhouse by *my* junior high peers: Hollis Todd who wore no underpants (I know, because he made no secret of it when he stood at the urinal next to me); Phillip Barnes, who was rivaled in uncouthness only by Hollis' sister Judy (who reportedly staged many fights herself with girls and guys); and Wayne Whitlock, a six foot one, eighth-grader, who could scale the ten-foot wall on the obstacle course using only one arm.

I remember riding home that night with my best friend Jimbo in the back seat of his Mother's station wagon. WSGN-AM, "The Big 610," was following up "Crimson and Clover" with "Honky Tonk Women."

"What did y'all think of the movie?" Jimbo's Mom cheerfully and optimistically asked.

"Oh, it was OK," we responded in unison which, if you understand teenage lingo, translated into: "It was beyond stupid, and thanks a lot for ruining another weekend night on this crap when we could have been at a party, attempting to kiss a girl or something."

"I thought it was really inspirational," she replied, hopefully. "You can take a lot of comfort and learn a lot of lessons from these movies!"

Sigh. No one but an adult would believe that Pat Boone could turn the hearts and minds of my hoodish peers who wouldn't even need the switchblades that I was sure they owned, but never saw in those early months of school.

However, I did see the Reid brothers, Saul and Paul, who were as distinct as fraternal twins can be.

Saul was sixteen when he re-entered the seventh grade. He had tattoos on both arms—faded-green 1969-era tattoos that I thought only cab drivers and filling station attendants dared. And Saul's muscles, so clearly defined that in semi-flex they rippled to such an extent that even class princess Rennie Robinson expressed wonder at them. These muscles seemed to discount Saul's needing a switchblade to keep us puny junior high pawns in our places. So full of swagger, with greased hair flipping up both in front and back, Saul held us all in contempt, and we held him in abject fear, complete and stupefying terror, but also with a strange and mesmerizing respect. For Saul, among other feats of scholastic daring, told everyone that Fridays were his day off, and after a few weeks, most teachers just skipped his name during Friday roll call. On the other days, instead of answering "Here," or "Present," Saul had his own cultural signifier: "Accounted for." And in some way that I didn't yet understand, he certainly was.

Truthfully, if you were smart, you did want Saul accounted for. During the first week of school, after having been exposed to Saul for maybe three days, I was sitting on the bleachers during gym class with my good friend Randy Manzella. Waiting for Coach Brewer to appear and so inform us of the remarkable feats of athletic prowess that we would be attempting this school year, Randy and I didn't account for Saul, who had slowly and imperceptibly crept closer to our row. Randy was no doubt filling my ears with yet another horror story he had heard about gym class—about boys popping your exposed rear with wet towels, or stealing your clothes as you showered. We vowed right then and there never to shower in gym class, and I suppose our false bravado set us up for Saul.

So sitting there, believing that our greatest problem concerned not appearing naked in the showers, we allowed Saul—that undulating cottonmouth—to strike. Except that Randy, God Bless him, wore thick glasses with wide black frames, and even Saul had a code. So it was I and I alone who qualified as Saul's prey. Up until this very moment, Saul and I had never spoken or even exchanged looks, or at least he had never caught me looking at him. Of course, everyone looked at Saul, just like everyone stares hypnotically at the reptile pit in the zoo, wondering just what prey continues to wriggle in that particular viper's throat.

So consider me the hamster.

"Hey, Candy-Ass!"

His voice conveyed no trace of anger, vitriol, or class-envy. His tone sounded the same pitch and inflection as all those "Accounted for's" we heard that year. Yet, the words themselves clearly communicated his menace.

"That's my spot, and if you don't get up by the time I count to ten, you're gonna get it."

And Saul showed me his flexed arm, which had extended from it at its the very end, not the switch-blade that had recently haunted my days and nights, but a massive, scarred fist. Displaying this prize, he began counting.

Each of us has a particular experience that gives special, personal meaning to the phrase "Words failed me." This, of course, was mine.

By this point—"three, four..." Randy and the entire Manzella family had set sail for their native Sicily. Actually, since he was the smartest kid in our class, Randy, with the encouraging words, "You better move," slid off his seat and found another, maybe five rows below us. Yet, hypnotized by Saul's viperous arm, I couldn't.

And so I wondered: Would a cross, at this late moment, make any difference at all? Would I stand a chance against the demon of my adolescence had I Pat Boone's smooth, silver-tongued delivery or his plasticine comb-over instead of my own frozen larynx and Beatle-bangs?

Good old Pat!

Would he ever be able to account for a viewer like me, the product of a mixed Protestant-Jewish family—a family who definitely did not own a cross?

I had seen crosses and actually touched a few in my time. My Dad worked in a jewelry store, and I had my first summer job there, just before this school year started. The store, Standard Jewelry Company, was in my Dad's family, so we were Jewish jewelers though no family name adorned any store signpost. And not only did we sell crosses, but crucifixes, and other jeweled Christian icons too. I knew that ordinary crosses were off-limits to me, but once I did ask Dad to get me a surfer's cross. My favorite male TV stars wore them, and so I assumed that girls would think they were cool. That these talismans also looked like the German Iron Cross escaped me then. Nevertheless, Dad got me the cross, which I then promptly gave to the girl-of-my-dreams, Joe's sister Mary Jane, who just as promptly handed it off to her little sister. Did this mean that I was going steady with a nine-year old named Margaret Lou?

But even if I hadn't given it away, Saul wouldn't have been impressed by it. Maybe I could have told him about the legend of the surfer's cross and the story of my unrequited love for the beautiful blonde-haired girl whom I watched in secret every day from my living room window. Maybe he was a closeted Jan and Dean surf-rock fan, for wasn't my story the stuff of every 60's teenage pop song? Maybe hearing my tragic lament, he would take pity on me or be so bored that he'd forget he was counting my fate.

These thoughts, though seemingly endless, had gotten us to the count of seven. My arm, Saul's intended target, was already beginning to ache.

But that's when the Pat Boone miracle happened.

Saul had just counted "eight," when the gym office door opened. Out from this inner sanctum strolled not a man in white bucks, but one in black cleats: Coach Billy "Bomber" Brewer, who was also an itinerant Baptist preacher. As the year went on, many guys in gym class would come to accuse "Bomber" of cheating, as he would call invisible fouls or interference whenever he had, or lost, the ball during the innumerable football and basketball games that composed most of our gym periods that year. On this day, however, the gym grew quiet, not so much because he was standing there, but because of what he had in his hand: A three-foot long, solid wood board, which, supposedly, he had named "The Little Bomber," after himself.

To this day I've never figured out how he knew what was transpiring ninety feet from his office without being able to see through those plaster walls. I suppose he knew that he had to account for Saul eventually and not let more than a couple of minutes go by without checking off his presence.

Whatever the case, Coach Brewer walked straight to us, never wavering, never looking elsewhere.

"Saul, get down here right now and grab those ankles!"

Saul, fist still poised above my already-wincing arm, had no excuse, no recourse.

So he complied. He descended the bleachers, walked right up to Coach, and bent over, grabbing those ankles in front of the entire gym class, God, and Pat Boone. Then "The Little Bomber" went to work. Three loud whacks that echoed like Bible thumps throughout the gym. To his credit, Saul held firm, and when Coach said "Get up, and go back to your seat," Saul did. But first, he extended his hand to "Bomber" and said, "Hey! They were good 'uns."

Saul left me alone after that. Oh, he might occasionally speak in my direction:

"You're fat, you know that?"

Of course, I did.

The only other encounter we had occurred during our class spelling bee trials. Since I was one of the champion class spellers, our teacher often allowed me to call out the words in practice sessions. On one particular afternoon, as I was anticipating which words those standing in line were bound to get, I saw Saul waiting his turn. My eyes skipped down the page to see the word he would be forced to spell.

When his turn came, I looked him in the eye and called it out: "CONVERSION, Saul."

"Conversion." He looked puzzled for a moment. Our eyes met again, and then he started:

"C-O-N-V-E-R-...

I waited, wondering. And hoping.

...S-I-O-N."

"That's right," I confirmed.

Saul neither smiled nor nodded. He merely took his place in the back of the line, waiting for his next word, or for the bell, or for something else that I would never understand. I wondered whether he was proud of himself, and if that pride might translate into something greater if he could just spell the next word correctly. I tried glancing down the list as my classmates struggled through "conversant" and "convoluted." But I didn't have a chance to see what would happen, for the bell for last period rang then, and we were off to the greater glories of Reading Lab or Machine Shop which is where I lost Saul each day. On this day, and this day only, I was actually a bit sad.

He never converted, by the way. Maybe in part because his brother Paul had reconstituted himself by Saul's standards into a "normal" student—meaning one who wanted to stick it out at least until high school.

And yes, before school officially released us for the summer, I saw Saul's switchblade. It was during science class. He had waited and waited, and finally, to impress Rennie Robinson, he brought it out, switched it open, and then, after maybe ten seconds, carefully closed it and returned it to his front left pocket. It was all rather anti-climatic, for by that point in the year, I had already experienced too much. I had even given a girl a box of candy for Valentine's Day: Debbie Patterson who was rail-skinny and had the longest, waviest blond hair I had ever seen, and who claimed to be part Cherokee.

"See how crooked my nose is? Just like an Indian!"

Two days after I gave her the candy she broke up with me because "I never called her."

It really didn't matter so much to me because at least I had one girlfriend in seventh grade.

Besides, when Saul showed me that menacing switchblade, he also did something else that he had never done before.

He called me by my name.

SWITCH

"That's how you open it, Terry."

Saul didn't make it to the end of that school year. He turned seventeen in April and so, as he pledged he would, he left us behind, journeying out into the Damascus of his life: A crossroads of glittering switchblade fame, a perpetual small-town rebellion.

It might make a nice, Hollywood ending if I said I never heard from or saw him again. That way I could leave him painted as defiant, plagued, and maybe even repentant, in an adult and rehabilitated life.

But I did see him again. It was three or four years later, my high school years. Shopping for Christmas at our local mall with my mother and brother, I looked up and coming out of WT Grant's, I saw a man and a woman pushing a baby stroller. The woman was a bleached blonde, a little heavy, but that could have been the after-effects of her pregnancy. I had never seen her before. But something looked familiar about the guy. He looked... would "beleaguered" be the right word? "Haunted?" I watched them for a minute as they strolled closer. And then I knew it was Saul. He had gained some weight. He had "settled," so to speak.

I imagined this little family taking their purchase from Grant's or Super-X Drugs home, and gathering that night in front of their Motorola watching "The Movie of the Week." Maybe they're eating burgers or Dinty Moore Stew. Maybe they have a beer or two and remember to give the baby his bottle. And maybe they keep the knives they cut their burgers with safely out of the baby's reach. I'd like to think so anyway.

I saw another movie unfold in those few moments, but I didn't stare too long. For I had seen crosses and switchblades in my small Alabama town. And I had survived them all.

14
A Warm Place to Laugh

Like most kids, I thought my parents married for love. Mom was nineteen, living at home with her widowed mother. Dad was twenty-six, living at home with his parents. One evening, my father's sister invited a girlfriend home for dinner. My father was sitting in the living room reading *The Birmingham News*. Their eyes met. He walked her home that night, and within a year they were married. The stuff dreams are made of.

But. And you surely knew something was coming, but was it this? Mom was Protestant (Methodist), and Dad was Jewish (Reform). When I discovered their truth at age seven, I still thought that love had brought them together. In relatively small-town Alabama in the early 1950's, what else could explain their union?

My parents were alternating social creatures. Alternating in the sense that my mother was and my father wasn't. Mom played in bridge clubs, gathered in garden clubs, enjoyed going out on the town with my father to movies, for dancing, or to eat at her favorite restaurants: Joy Young, a Chinese-American place on one of downtown Birmingham's busiest streets, or The Bright Star, a Greek-owned establishment that had been central to Bessemer since 1907. Dad indulged my Mom in these social settings, but they were never for him. He preferred a good football or baseball game. Mainly though, he loved sitting in "his chair" in front of the TV, centrally located in our den. He loved it if we watched his favorite shows—"Combat," "The Rifleman," "Cheyenne"—with him. But then, he seemed to love it just as much if we holed up in other parts of the house and left him in front of the TV alone.

After supper, though, both of my parents loved sitting on our front porch, sometimes joined by neighbors, but mainly just with my grandmother, as they watched my brother and I playing chase or "Red Light" or some form of "ball" in the yard. Our street was old and established in the hills just south of the main business district. In the daylight savings time hours before dark, couples from adjoining streets would stroll past, waving hello, sometimes stopping for a quick bit of gossip, in the way I imagined they did in all the years before I was born.

"Who was that?" became my most often-asked question, and though it scarcely mattered whether I knew them or remembered them later, discovering the names of some of these couples satisfied me in a way I couldn't describe, especially if they had names like Frank and Estelle Sachs, or Isidore and Esther Bach.

In the adult world, the only "single" people I knew were my grandmother's friends, all widows like her. There was one lone widower on our street, Mr. Hollingsworth, but he lasted just about six months before he found love again in the arms of Mrs. Davis, one of my grandmother's good church friends.

So somehow a woman living by herself, while sad, wasn't strange to me. But a man? Well, I could never visualize my Dad being alone, without women, even though my Mom often referred to him as "a loner." Still, until Edward walked into my life, I didn't truly know what a loner was. I first saw him when I was eleven or twelve, standing in our front doorway being greeted by my mother and grandmother as if he were returning from some foreign war. They ushered him into the kitchen, sliced him a piece of homemade pound cake, poured him a coke over ice, and then introduced me.

My grandmother called me by my own invented nickname, "Bob," as did my brother and father and maid, Dissie. They were the only ones, though, until Edward came.

"Hello Bobby, ha ha ha ha ha ha ha."

He always laughed that way: a louder form of chuckling but not as maniacal as Batman's Joker.

On this early summer evening, I stood there quietly, watching Edward, and waiting. And then my Dad walked in.

"Why, hello Edward! Where have you been?"

Where indeed?

I never heard exactly where Edward had been, but I did learn that Edward was an old family friend who had gone to high school with my mother, that his own parents still lived nearby on Dartmouth Avenue, and that Edward was once again living with them. That seemed strange to me: a man in his late thirties still living with his parents. It almost distracted me enough to forget that The Johnny Cash TV show had already started, but I caught myself in enough time to get to Johnny.

Edward stayed for a few hours that night, eventually joining us in the den and trying to make conversation with me while Johnny and his guests—maybe Dylan or Neil Young—performed songs on live television before the days of VCR: before the time when if you missed something you could watch your recording later in the privacy of your own company. He couldn't just watch, though. He had to try to fit in with us, with me:

"Bobby, ha ha ha. Do you like The Buckinghams?"

Actually, I did own a Buckinghams' 45: "Hey Baby (They're Playing Our Song)." I hadn't intended buying it. I wanted the new Paul Revere and the Raiders hit in its picture sleeve cover. I trusted Pizitz, our downtown department store, but when I got the record home and pulled it from its sleeve, there were The Buckinghams instead. But the song sounded fine and became a favorite on my portable turntable.

"Yeah, they're OK."

"Ha ha ha ha ha."

Over the next three years, Edward would usually visit in two-to-three week intervals, though sometimes a couple of months would go by between visits. He never explained where he had gone, what he had been doing, and whenever we asked my Mom if she knew, she just shook her head:

"I have no idea where that man is. Why would I know?"

During these first visits, though (the "honeymoon phase" I might call it now), he'd drive the six blocks from his parents' house in his old gold Mustang. Edward's old gold car matched his cigarette brand, as well as the golden aura from his slick brown hair, neatly parted and combed to the left; his complexion, a gold-tinted facial rosacea; and even his teeth, stained golden from those smokes and his admitted coffee addiction. In the fall weather, he'd wear a gold cardigan. A sweater that had seen better days, which, I suppose, summed up Edward's life, too.

Sometimes, he'd take us places, like the zoo or the Birmingham A's baseball game at Rickwood Field. Since these outings usually took place on weekdays while my Dad was at work or Saturday afternoons when he ritually mowed our lawn, Dad never went on these trips, only Edward and my mother or grandmother, and my brother Mike. From the back I'd see Edward stretch his long arm across the bucket seat and rest it on the back of my mother's seat. I'd hear him call her "honey." And my mother never moved away from him or seemed to notice or mind at all. But my Dad never called her "honey." When I was younger, I did hear them call each other "Poohlard" which I supposed was their personal term of endearment, though I had no idea what "Poohlard" meant, what it referred to, or who came up with it in the first place. What I was sure of, though, was that it was no "honey."

Once, Edward's nephew Billy, a guy maybe a year older than me, came to visit. On one of these car trips, Billy turned to me and, nodding at the grown ups in front, said,

"It's like they're married or something."

While Billy's words numbed me into silence, I had to admit to myself that it did kind of feel like that. For a while during that summer I wondered, and waited, and became increasingly nervous and uncomfortable at the regularity and frequency of Edward's visits.

For a period in that first fall, Edward's visits became weekly events. Soon, he and my mother began spending whole days together shellacking thick old boards with magazine art and then displaying them for sale at art shows throughout the upper portion of our state. They never had great success, but at one show, a kid my age literally bounced from booth to booth proudly holding for all to see the shellacked Guru that he bought from Edward. Edward was pleased, too, and for a time, he and my mother tried to give all their boards a 60's theme with collages and "mod" patterns cut from old *Look*, *Life*, and even my father's stash of *Playboy* magazines.

I tried to tell myself that the fact my mother was travelling with another man meant nothing to our world. And since no one else discussed it, seemed to mind it, or acted strangely about it, I was pretty much able to still my fantasies and worries. Dad, my brother Mike, and I would sometimes join them in mid-travel too, and to my memory, nothing in these art tours seemed amiss. Everyone got along well, though Dad never really "got" the art and was usually interested only in whether Mom's sales defrayed her expenses.

In fact, that she spent a lot of quality time with Edward never really bothered Dad. In the realm of romance, my Dad wasn't a valiant lover, a man to make women swoon. He worked in a wholesale jewelry store, and for all anniversaries, birthdays, and Christmas presents, he gave my mother a carefully or hastily selected ring or pendant or necklace. Sometimes she liked the pieces; just as often she didn't. And sometimes she vowed he gave her the same item that he had given her the year before.

For other than calling each other "Poohlard," my parents

never spoke in endearments. And they rarely touched each other even casually. Once, in the backseat of a fancy Cadillac, I heard my grandmother telling one of her widowed friends that my mother " just wasn't kissable." I thought my grandmother was wrong then. But in reality, I think she knew more than I knew about my parents' world of love.

So Dad didn't complain about Edward. In fact, the only thing that seemed to bother him about Edward during the entire time we knew him was that when he dropped in on us at night—always unannounced—it was never earlier than 8:30 or 9:00. Dad would grumble at the sound of the doorbell:

"Who can that be?"

But at that time of night, we all knew who it could be. Dad would walk into his closet next to the den, and somehow in a space no bigger than a phone booth, change from his pajama bottoms to a pair of house pants, and then trudge to the door to let Edward back into our lives. Edward would plop down in my grandfather's favorite chair and join whatever conversation or TV show we were engaged in. If it were a baseball game, Edward would try to participate in the action, though he didn't seem to quite get our American pastime. I can hear him clearly, even now, asking Dad:

"Alvin, ha ha ha, do they still bunt?"

"Yeah Edward, they bunt when they need to," Dad said as if he were trying to explain the intricacies of the Phillips screwdriver to an amnesia victim.

Edward always stayed past my 10:00 bedtime, and I'd have to give him a hug too on my way to bed.

"Good night Bobby, ha ha ha ha ha."

Sometimes he'd keep my parents up until 11:30.

"Doesn't he realize that some of us have to work," Dad would ask at supper the next night.

But no one had an answer, and no one ever asked Edward to change his ways.

After these first few months, there came the less normal occasions: arrivals on cold and rainy nights minus that gold mustang. Sometimes I would get to the door first. Turning on the porch light, I'd see Edward standing there. His face would brighten with the light, so glad he was to see us. My mother would escort him in to his accustomed chair by the wall heater. As I looked him over on those nights, I thought Edward's face had grown thinner and redder. His eyes looked kind of dark and sunken. And I couldn't see how his thin black trench coat and undersized umbrella could possibly keep him warm and dry during his strolls in those winter rains. Nor could I understand why he'd get out on such evenings in the first place just to walk the streets.

"Is he crazy," Dad asked.

"I don't know," Mom offered. "I guess he's just lonely."

And when he'd leave late on those nights, he wouldn't head home. My mother sort of confessed this one day when she and my grandmother were lamenting what to do about Edward.

"I think he goes on to Rowan's house," I heard Mom say.

Rowan was yet another single man, one who lived two blocks from us in an old Victorian house with his mother. Rowan was our pediatrician, a man Edward's age who had also gone to high school with my mother.

"What does he do there, and why does he go so late," I asked.

But my mother wouldn't speculate with me. I was only thirteen or fourteen, and she figured that I was either too young or simply didn't need to know about the wanderings of grown men.

Despite my early wonderings about him, I always liked Edward. He was nice to me, to all of us. His visits were inconvenient, true, but at some point, he seemed like another member of the family, sitting in his chair, folding into this warm and friendly place to be.

And then, just like he appeared, suddenly one day he never

came back. I was toiling in high school angst by then, so I had forgotten about him mainly, but my brother Mike hadn't. Maybe a year after Edward's last appearance, Mike asked if anyone had heard from Edward or knew what he was doing.

"I think he's working in Birmingham," my mother said. "I hear he's the night clerk at the Redmont Hotel."

The Redmont, where we spent the night years before during a winter power outage. The Redmont which, like Joy Young and most of downtown Birmingham, had gone to seed since the boycotts back in the 60's. The Redmont, full of tricks, and treats, and now Edward.

Things happen as you get older. Things change in ways you never thought they would. On breaks from college and grad school, I'd find myself at my parents' house, sleeping till noon, and then preparing to go clubbing but never earlier than ten o'clock.

"Where are you going at this time of night," my Dad invariably asked.

"Out. To a club. Dancing." Why was he bothering me? Why did he find this strange?

"It's time for bed," he'd say, shaking his head. I'm sure we both wondered a little about the other, then. He'd look over at Mom who, while surely worried about my staying out so late, nevertheless seemed to stare back at me with a little longing, a little envy. But even then, in those moments between my parents and me, I never thought of Edward. Not once. That is, not until I saw him again on one of those late nights.

At the dance club.

I'm sitting at the bar of this downtown Birmingham club with my friend Sarah. We're taking a break from the throngs of dancers and watchers, and from all those who do both at the same time. I hear the thumping bass of Thelma Houston's "Don't Leave Me This Way" a long corridor away. I'd love to catch up to its plaintive cries, and am about to suggest that we head back. I take another swallow of beer and then look across the bar to where several older men are sipping whiskey and talking. The bartender slides away just at that instant, and I see one of these men more clearly. From that distance he looks the same, golden, and for a second I think about going over to speak. But I don't want to see him in close-up now, and besides, it seems very late. It seems time for us to head home, to the places where we can go: the places where we're wanted and loved.

I know I didn't, but part of me swears that as we left that night, I heard laughter trailing behind me. And my name following me home.

15
In Its Infancy

We were on vacation when it died. My friends told me on our return about the funeral, about how Hank and Jo Ellen cried and hugged them and thanked them all for being there.

"It was just so *sad*," Carol said, as if this were a question. As if *it* was still the question.

"Yeah, but it would have been sadder had it lived," Jane added.

I felt bad that I missed the ceremony because I had been the most supportive of our group during the last weeks, calling and visiting them frequently. So the day we returned I walked the two and a half blocks from my house over to Hank and Jo Ellen's apartment at Clarendon Manor. Hank opened the door, just as before, just as if this were an ordinary visit.

"Buddy. Come in. We were..."

"No, I can't stay, but I wanted to see you and tell you how sorry I am for..." And that stopped me. Which word should I use before "death," I wondered. But Hank saved me:

"Thanks Buddy." And he even smiled. "We appreciate it. You sure you won't come in? No? OK, I'll tell Jo Ellen. See you on Sunday."

Sure enough, the following Sunday there he was at church, shepherding our youth group—the bunch of us he'd volunteered to manage four months earlier. He'd set up a Ping Pong table outside our Sunday school classroom when he first took over and encouraged us to come early. What he never counted on, though, was the difficulty through those weeks in getting us to put down our paddles and come to Jesus. His call became familiar and so tired: "Let's go group!" Increasingly, and to a teenaged person, we'd smirk and roll our eyes. After he turned his back, Jane would mock him, "Let's go group," in that way that only an adolescent girl can reduce a grown man to complete impotency in the eyes of her peers.

Hank and Jo Ellen weren't like our former youth directors, Dick and Laura, who played James Taylor and Carole King records for us. Dick and Laura had "mentored" us for eighteen months at their house on Dartmouth Avenue, an old wood and brick parsonage with wide rooms and a jungle for a back yard. We didn't confine our "Dick and Laura" visits to only Sunday nights for youth group. They told us to come by anytime. For teenagers, a refuge with cool, hip people who let them bring, and even bought them, beer...well, I guess we thought this was natural. Or at least we never questioned if it wasn't. I had my first full beer—Miller Malt—at their house, and I was barely fifteen. I wonder how any of us, especially Dick and Laura, thought this arrangement could last. How we couldn't see or even anticipate the storm that was coming to our little Alabama community at all.

The storm that turned into a deluge once Laura decided that mentoring us wasn't enough.

When it broke in the spring of my sophomore year, the impact truly made the earth move under our feet. I'll never know exactly how our parents discovered that Laura had seduced my friend Ray-Ray. I'm guessing that his folks started wondering about the lengthy phone calls and the even lengthier afternoon hours at Dick and Laura's. I guess it finally dawned on them that it wasn't healthy for a fifteen year-old boy to be actively seeking out the company of a twenty-two year-old mother of two. And when our leaders finally acted, the debris left in our former youth leaders' wake would be collected for decades in the form of bitter feelings and mistrust from all sides.

A bitterness and mistrust that almost cost me my best friend. But that's not the story I want to tell here.

After the revelation, the church elders quietly asked Dick and Laura to move. We would still see Dick in the corridors and class-rooms of our school, though, for he had been and would continue to be our beloved Humanities teacher.

We, of course, had no choice in the matter, though at the time our indignant minds thought we should have. The church elders began a more careful youth director screening process then, and their search turned up a young couple new to our congregation: Hank and Jo Ellen. After they were hired, a few in our group were invited to a dessert party to introduce ourselves. Hank said we could call him "Hank" on that night, but I noticed that then and always, his wife referred to him as "Henry."

Hank worked in Sears' shoe department, and you can in-fer what you will about that. I know we did. He was eternally cheerful, and unlike Dick who wore leather sandals, enjoyed fine literature and opera, and who was a Tulane grad, Hank wore half-sleeve dress shirts, clip-on ties, sidewalls above his ears. And compared to the VW bus that Dick bought and drove especially to cart us around, Hank drove a Dodge Dart "Swinger," just like the one the elderly receptionist at my Dad's office drove. Hank's and Jo Ellen's apartment smelled like stale lime Kool-Aid, too, and they never played music for us, though they did let us come swimming in the complex's pool.

For the first eight weeks we knew them, we tried to make our arrangement work. I think the main thing that kept us all going was that Jo Ellen looked every bit the seven months pregnant that she was. A quiet woman, she never had performed on stage as Laura had. She never professed to liking Carly Simon or Rita Coolidge either. And once, when I sat down by her as Sunday evening service was beginning, she got up and moved to the other side of Henry. I'm sure now that she was overwhelmed by the changes in her life and what was to come for her and Hank. I know that we all watched and waited with her for the baby to come. Even teens know the excitement of a new baby.

Even teens can feel empathy, at least for short periods of time.

My mother was the one who broke the news to me. It was just like her to tell me without mincing words, without worrying about their effect, just as she had done when she informed me that the church had fired Dick and Laura:

"Y'all won't be going to their house anymore. Imagine a woman like that around young boys. I knew it too when she and Dick came to supper that time. She had nothing to say to me, and when one woman can't talk to another woman, well, that tells you something. She only had eyes for you boys!"

They were hard words to digest. This time as my mother spoke, however, I couldn't even swallow. I had nothing to say, no fresh wounds to protect, no friend to defend:

"Hank and Jo Ellen's baby came all right, if you can call it that. There's something wrong with it, but they don't know what exactly. It has water on the brain, and fluid all in its lungs. But what's worse is that the doctors can't tell whether it's a boy or a girl."

I sat at our kitchen table as I listened to this, surrounded by geometry problems. I didn't understand it then, and in some ways I still don't. I know nature has a will, and though we might take all necessary precautions, we can't control the circumstances of childbirth—or what happens when one person's chromosomes mix with another's. What I do know is that when the time came, my wife had ultrasounds and the best pre-natal care we could afford. But it was only when I saw both of my daughter's healthy and whole bodies in front of me, pink and raw, that I stopped worrying that something would go wrong, that something would be wrong. That what happened to Hank and Jo Ellen would happen to us.

As in any small town, word passed down quickly about the baby: That regardless of the circumstances, Hank and Jo Ellen still wanted people to visit, including the teenagers of their youth group.

"But will we have to *see* the baby," we wondered, "and if we do, what will we do? What should we say?"

I had no practice in witnessing this sort of distress, the awkward reality of the dying or the abnormal. When I was nine or ten, on a certain route we always took driving through town, we'd pass a house where a water-brained, mongoloid boy lived. I don't know if "water-brained" or "mongoloid" are even accurate terms for him, but those are the words my mother used back then. He had weird, elongated fingers too. Somehow, I even know that his name was Rene. Such a big head he had, and the blackest hair. He always stood on the street corner and either I or my brother or our friend Robert would shout at him as we passed, as if he were a post or a dog or a lightning-cleft tree. He'd wave or cry or groan at us, and try to smile, Rene would. And one day, he just wasn't there anymore. I have no idea what happened to him, and for a long time I forgot about him too.

Not too long before the turn of events with Hank and Jo Ellen, my grandmother suffered a string of strokes and lay dying in her nursing home during that summer when I turned fifteen. "I don't want you to see her like this," my mother said in some semblance of protective instinct. So I quit going to see her. The last time I saw her she knew me and showed me her "progress," as she termed it: the six or eight inches she could slide up and down her bed.

And fourteen years ago when my father passed, though I visited him as he lay in a coma, I chose not to look at his corpse lying in that unadorned Jewish coffin. I don't know any longer what these decisions say about me or whether they were right or wrong. They simply were.

Just like my decision to visit Jo Ellen and Hank after they brought their baby home. We're sitting in their living room. Jo Ellen has the baby in her arms, swaddled tightly to prevent any chance that I might see its ungendered region. She's feeding the baby its bottle. It drinks greedily as babies do. Its head is twice the size it should be, the pulsing blue veins running throughout more noticeable than you'd believe they could be. It has pale blue eyes, though of course they have no focus to them. Halfway through the feeding as I stare intently at this scene, the baby spits up all the milk, as many babies also do.

Jo Ellen apologizes for it and tries to wipe it all away. I feel like I'm in the way, so I apologize, too, and tell her I have to be somewhere. As Hank walks me to the door, though, I hear his baby start crying. It's a sound I've never heard before. How do I describe it? A high-pitched hoarseness? A wail? A tin door scraping in the wind?

After that afternoon, I never went back. I never saw the baby again. It lived for another few weeks. They always knew it would die in a matter of days, yet they continued caring for it, feeding it, changing it, and God knows, putting it down to sleep at night, until the end.

If my memory is right, Hank and Jo Ellen never named this child, or if they did, they never told us. I guess there are certain barriers in every experience: the ones you just can't bring yourself to cross.

And unfortunately, another of those barriers was the one that existed between this couple and our youth group. I'd like to say that their tragedy brought us closer, but I can't because it didn't. Each Sunday morning, he'd call "Let's go group," and each Sunday fewer and fewer of us were there to respond. And those who were there chafed every step of the way. By my junior year in high school when most of us could drive, we'd leave the evening church service before youth group and drive away to Pasquale's, our local pizza joint, to eat and carelessly socialize as we liked to do. At some point that year or the next, Hank and Jo Ellen moved out of our town. The Sears store where Hank worked at our pathetic little mall closed. Two years later, the entire mall was converted into a grocery store or something, but by then Hank and Jo Ellen were barely a memory for any of us.

It's strange to think now of this couple we often made fun of; this couple we chose to abandon. We had cruel nicknames for them too. Him, we called "Winky-Dink," a variation on his last name. For Jo Ellen, we didn't so much have a nickname as an adjectival descriptor; she was always "the beautiful and vivacious Jo Ellen" to us. And, I will confess, these cruelties came after they lost their child.

They must be in their late 60's now. Are they still together? Are they still alive? Did they ever have another baby? Or are they grandparents now? What do they remember about those days in our town, in Bessemer? Do they remember them as lost? As horrible? Did they ever get over the child who shouldn't have lived but for a time did? Do they remember the names they surely considered for that child when they knew they were expecting? A boy's name, and a girl's?

And if they remember those days as vividly as I do, do they see us, the teenagers in the church youth group who looked so eager and trusting on that first night? The ones who came to visit; the ones who came to the funeral; and the ones who, after a brief period of mourning, decided they wanted nothing more to do with them?

I wonder now if they ever forgave us for all that we did. For all that we weren't, and were. Or did they successfully bury us in Bessemer, too, on the day they left, quietly, completely, and with no forwarding address?

16
A View from the Seats

Why am I sitting underneath the upper deck in Birmingham's Legion Field with Alan Crosby? You'd think we really like each other or something. It's a freezing December night—the night of the Florence-Jax State football game, two lesser college teams playing for a Shriner's charity.

Alan's Daddy, wearing his Shriner fez, is sitting with Alan's mother across from us on the press box side of the stands along with the 200 or so other fans that have bothered to attend. I'm betting that no one here knows these teams' records or who is supposed to win. I decide to pull for Jax State because they're wearing red. Alan doesn't care, and after the first quarter, neither of us is paying much attention to the game, partly because Alan keeps telling me weird stories about what he might do to a girl if he ever gets one, and partly because he keeps pointing to his mother and daddy across the way, so far from us that they look like semi-colored dots on the far right side of a Van Gogh painting.

He keeps cussing his "old man," the man who brought us to the game. The man who paid for our tickets, and bought us Shoney's Big Boy hamburgers beforehand which Alan and I ate with gusto.

The man who doesn't know as I do that his fourteen year-old son is a known pot dealer.

But the other reason I quit watching this game is that football is sacred to me, and I want to pretend that this isn't a real game. As a good southern boy, I treat college football with more reverence than I ever have a church service, and for the first nineteen years of my life, I was at least a decent Methodist. In truth, however, my main goal while attending morning services every Sunday was to sit on the back row by one of the teenaged girls and mark the rituals of the service through feeling the various parts of her leg. By contrast, I've never felt a girl's leg during a college football game, nor do I want to. Even now I forget to caress my wife's shoulder when she's sitting right by me during an Alabama Crimson Tide game.

But on this night it's just Alan and I, two noticeably uncaring fourteen year-olds sitting by ourselves in a barren part of a stadium that on Alabama game days fills to 72,000. I don't smoke pot yet, though ten years later, on the weekend before I return to grad school at the University of Tennessee, I'll be sitting pretty much in this same seat, stoned out of my mind, trying to keep track of Ray Perkins' debut as Alabama head coach. Bama will unimpressively defeat Georgia Tech that warm September day, but I won't remember anything about the game except where I'm sitting and the hazy view I had of teams in Crimson and Old Gold.

Tonight, Alan has managed to acquire a pack of Swisher Sweet cigars, and though I feel illicit and immoral, I puff along with him as he continues to ridicule his "old man," his father.

"He's such a dumbass! He actually thinks I wanted to come to this game, that it would be fun. The stupid bastard! I don't know what I'd have done if you hadn't come with me."

I've known the Crosbys all my life, and Mr. Crosby has always treated me well. Usually, he seems happy, even jovial. But then I have no idea what goes on behind the closed doors of the Crosby house in Lakewood, Bessemer's most prestigious neighborhood.

Alan is the first child I've known to be adopted. In fact, it's only through him that I learned about this procedure. He knew he was adopted, too, and what that did to him through the years is anyone's guess. What it did to me, though, finding out from my mother on the day she took me to his fourth birthday party that Mr. and Mrs. Crosby weren't Alan's real parents...Well, the best I can say is that I don't remember the party too well. I do remember that every time I looked at Alan, all I could see was a boy someone gave away.

I'll let the psychologists argue over whether a boy of four can feel empathy. Maybe what I was feeling then was pure relief that I wasn't Alan, a feeling I had every time I saw him. Not that I saw or thought about him often during the following years. By the time I reached junior high, any empathy I had for Alan was buried by attempts to avoid him, after I learned that he was the one selling pot to my friends, that he was one of those boys my mother had warned me about:

"I just don't trust that..." and you could fill in the name of the boy she claimed "just didn't know right from wrong."

Yet, she never named Alan because while she might have thought he was a little different, maybe even a little odd, she loved his mother and thought so well of his family. That nothing that bad could ever exist in their midst.

It's unsettling to know such a family secret at age thirteen, but I couldn't tell her what I knew about the Crosbys, and how I felt. That I knew Alan shouldn't be trusted.

So I wondered as I sat in Legion Field that evening why I agreed to go. I no longer remember whether he asked me himself, or had his mother call my mother. Maybe both happened. Nevertheless, on the day he asked, she agreed and I agreed:

"I'm so glad you're going with the Crosbys to the game," Mom said. "Alan needs a friend. His mother is such a sweet woman."

And as I'm replaying my mother's words, sitting on this cold metal backless stadium bench, Alan leans into me, points his middle finger out towards the fans huddled on the other side, and announces as loudly as he can to the seats on the east side of the stadium that that "sweet woman" sitting way over there is nothing but a "STUPID BITCH!"

I look closely, but none of those dots stirs at all.

When the game ends and we rejoin them, the dumb bastard and stupid bitch buy us hot chocolate and then drive us to The Spinning Wheel for dessert. On the way there, Alan tells his Dad to put on WSGN, the Big 610. His Dad cheerfully complies. A song I've never quite understood is playing:

So, he starts his rappin'
Hopin' something will happen...
He's got you where he wants you...
you've gotta face reality...

For the rest of the ride, I go very quiet and still.

I lie in bed that night unable to sleep, thinking about Alan, his parents, and still tasting that stupidly sweet cigar. I knew I'd never agree to go anywhere with Alan again, no matter what my mother said. No matter how sweet Alan's mother is.

At that fourth birthday party when I discover he's adopted, Alan is wearing a cowboy outfit, complete with red hat, black shirt with silver sequins, and a gun holster around his waist. Yet maybe I have it wrong. Maybe I'm the cowboy that day.

While I might not remember what we wore, what I'll never forget is that Alan's mouth hangs perpetually open. At age four, I don't know the phrase "mouth-breather," but that's what Alan is. When he says anything, even a simple "Hey," it sounds as if he has that horrible congestive cold I had the week before. I ask Mom about the way Alan talks, and she tells me that he has an "adenoidal problem."

"What?" I'm even more confused. Adults say such foreign things as if you've been speaking their language for decades, instead of for the two-plus years you've been able to string together the few words you can. Mom doesn't notice my wonder and simply goes on talking to Mrs. Holt as if I'm not there. It's weeks later that she finally explains that unlike me, Alan didn't have his adenoids removed:

"They took yours out at the same time they removed your tonsils," she clarifies.

But I'm still not so clear.

"Why didn't they take his out," I ask, because leaving something so ugly-sounding as adenoids in a kid's mouth must either be a mistake or a sign that his parents don't know what's best for him.

Mom doesn't know why, though, and for the rest of the years I know Alan, he'll always sound underwater; he'll always hang his mouth open no matter whether he's smiling, upset, or about to tell another lie. The hanging mouth gives him a dull look usually, except when he's lying or about to hatch another plan to drive his old bastard crazy.

Then, his eyes brighten. But what I really feel at those times is that his eyes go just a bit crazy.

I keep thinking about those crazy eyes now, and as I've been asking my old friends about their memory of Alan, I find this out: on the street in Lakewood where he lived, he wasn't the only adopted child. Two other households did likewise, and no one can say now which adoption turned out the worst.

The Palmer's adopted son, Ralph, once fell out of the balcony of Birmingham's Ritz Theater when he was twelve or thirteen. That time he survived. A few years later, he joins our Methodist Youth Fellowship supper one Sunday night. The adults have supplied us with buckets of KFC, and Ralph keeps handling the jug of gooey brown gravy:

"I'll give anyone who drinks this entire jug $10," he proclaims, and plunks a ten right on our table.

When we all just stare at him, he plunks down another five: "Make it fifteen, but you have to drink it all!"

This is 1969, and I've never had fifteen dollars at one grasp in my whole life. But not even that fact can motivate me, or anyone else, to drink that viscous burnt umber sludge.

Ralph chuckles, puts his money back in his wallet, and leaves us, supposedly for a date he has with a woman we don't know. Ten or fifteen years later, on his second marriage, he's out on his boat and falls again. This time from a heart attack, and this time, he doesn't make it back.

In one of those biological breakthroughs, after adopting Ralph, the Palmers go on to birth a daughter of their own, proving only that nature can never be understood either.

Further down this street, the Foote family adopted three children. I don't know the oldest two, but the youngest, Sally, is in my kindergarten class along with Alan and my neighborhood friends Mary Jane, Ted, and Elise. It's clear even to us that Sally's five-year old wildness isn't normal. I remember her getting into trouble almost every day: talking, getting out of her seat, chasing Keith McDougal with a pair of scissors, and possibly even biting Ted Clark's ear.

My mother kept our class photo, and when I drag it out now, I see that Sally is smiling. How did we all know then, and why do I remember so well today, that when we saw that smile, we knew to run from it? That it was an evil we couldn't name?

On the other end from Sally, you can also spot Alan by his open mouth. Somehow, everyone else disappears in their presence, though after that year, when we disperse into our assigned public schools, Sally will be the one to disappear from my life, except in the gossip-stories I'll hear, the rumors I'll never know for sure to be true.

Like the rumor spread by Alan himself that when they are teenagers, he and Sally have sex in a tent he set up in his backyard. Maybe Sally would have confirmed the story if anyone had followed her or cared enough to ask. But by then, no one paid attention, much less cared, about anything Alan said.

Sally's father was superintendent of the Bessemer school system during those years. And then one year, he wasn't. I don't know what happened other than they moved away, and whether it was because of Sally or not, the reality is that they went someplace where for a little while anyway, no one knew who they were.

After kindergarten, Alan and I didn't attend the same school until high school, and that was only for the first two years. He had a reputation by then as a liar and a dealer.

At some point in junior high, everyone starts calling him "Big Al," the name I discover later that refers to his schizo-druggie alternate persona. I find out about his dealing in eighth grade on the night I sleep over at Ray-Ray's. Our friend Corky is there too, and after supper and maybe four games of Monopoly, Ray-Ray and Corky beckon me to follow them through the basement door and out to the woods behind Ray-Ray's house.

"Now," Ray-Ray says, "you don't have to do this with us, but you're not gonna stop us or tell on us either, right?"

And he proceeds to fire up a joint which he and Corky pass between them for the next several minutes. Ray-Ray gets very stoned, or at least it seems so through my uninitiated eyes. He starts running through the woods, shouting "Lord Cheops grant me mercy!"

When he isn't stoned, Ray-Ray tends to read on the mythological side of adolescent lit.

Corky catches my eye and keeps looking straight into me.

"Hey, I don't feel a thing."

But he's smiling now and not moving a muscle.

I don't know what's supposed to happen, or what we're going to do with Ray-Ray.

"Where did you guys get this stuff," I ask.

"Where do you think," Corky says. "From Big Al."

Lord Cheops doesn't appear this night, and eventually Ray-Ray calms down enough for Corky and me to lead him back to his house, where he climbs in bed and begins pleasantly snoring.

For weeks after, whenever I see Corky, he brightens and says, "Eye-Eye," our code for Ray-Ray's pronouncement deep into that woodsy night:

"I'm so HIGH!"

A year later when Alan turns up in my Biology class, I wonder what else, what *more* he possesses.

It's 1970, and most of us guys, even in small-town Alabama, sport longer hair. Mine is in Beatle-Bangs, and Ray-Ray's black waves are parted down the middle. The ninth grade girls fall all over him, which is only funny when you consider the deeper truth about him that he'll only reveal after he graduates. Alan's hair, though, is a mass of kinky curls, and when he grows it out, it resembles an untamed flying wedge.

Unlike with Ray-Ray, no girl falls for me. I won't even be kissed properly until I'm in eleventh grade. I don't know about Alan. Girls seem to go for dangerous guys, but he's a breed beyond danger. In Biology class, Kay Rodgers sits by him willingly. She moved to our school earlier this year and has already successfully navigated her way into the best girl's club and into the exalted ranks of freshman cheerleading. She's also a devout member of Youth for Christ.

So why is she sitting next to Alan, whispering to him, laughing with him, touching his arm?

When I look at them, their desk-seats pulled so close together, I believe they're a couple, though supposedly Kay is dating a senior at another school.

What is the biology of this: a Youth for Christ girl consorting with a known mouth-breathing, wedge-headed pot dealer?

"The biggest jerks always get the best girls," Ray-Ray says. Later in life, I'll translate this line into "We accept the love we think we deserve." But right now, Ray-Ray himself can have Lisa or Melissa or Theresa. Yet he warns me to stay away from Alan.

Alan's family lived next door to Corky's. You can't say the two were best friends, but since each had a crazy wild streak as wide as 19th Street, Bessemer's busiest shopping artery, they couldn't help but find each other on late summer nights.

Or any night really when they needed some trouble.

They disregarded bedtimes and curfews. All Corky had to do to escape his parents' confines was to climb out his ground-level bedroom window. With Alan, I'm not certain of the set-up, since in my memory, I never entered his house, much less his room, after age four. Whereas Corky's parents, who had raised three kids before him, seemed "over" the duties of yet another wild son—his two older brothers having formed a hard rock band named variously The Trojans, Night Wind, and Mother Savage—Alan's caring parents somehow trusted him. According to Alan, they went to bed by 8:30 or 9 each night, believing that Alan was in his room, studying.

Corky would take the family car without permission when he was fifteen, and drive it hell-bent over Woodland Hills and through Thomas Acres. He'd wreck it, burn out the transmission, and get pulled over by troopers three or four times a year. And on all of these occasions, he'd be drinking heavily, for unsurprisingly, Bessemer had several convenience outlets for underage and unlicensed kids to buy beer and Boone's Farm.

Once, stopped by a trooper after having consumed several pitchers of draft beer at Shakey's Pizza Parlor—a joint situated in the same plaza as Shoney's Big Boy—Corky tried walking a line and talking his way out of a cell:

"But Ocifer, I only had two beers at Shokey's."

Corky was audacious-wild. Years later at a friend's bachelor party held at Sammy's A-Go-Go, I suggested to Corky that he could out-dance the strippers who kept showing up at our table. Without a pause, Corky mounted the table and began his singular gyrations. I think someone slipped him a ten, too.

Alan, though, was reckless-wild. How does a thirteen year-old make drug contacts? Where does he find them? And that recklessness coupled with his parents' trust? Well, Alan didn't have to sneak his parents' car out; they bought him his first when he was fifteen, on the day he got his permit. A new Chevy Malibu. Nothing could go wrong there.

But when it did, they got him a newer one.

Alan spent most of these times alone. I don't think any of us really grasped the places he visited, the sights he saw. The dark adventures he experienced.

There were times when even Corky decided to stay out of Alan's way.

"That fucker is crazy," he'd say.

Still, they had their after-hours parties where, according to Corky, they'd "drink up a couple of cases of Big M (Miller Malt)," and get so drunk they'd pass out. "And when we came to, we just started drinking again."

At this point in their stories, we might also hear about the elementary school's broken windows, or that its kitchen had been raided and was now short of many of its staples. Or, we might notice the faded green water tower, hundreds of feet tall, right at the entrance to the high school. Over one November week-end, someone had climbed it and with a gallon of white paint, inscribed the legend "Peterson's Perverts" on the side facing the school. Peterson was our principal, Horace Peterson, who liked to make regular morning announcements over the intercom. Periodically, he liked to denounce the "perverts" who had strewn the school lawn with cigarette butts or spray-painted the drive leading to the school doors.

Using a term like "perverts" over a high school intercom, of course, could only incite all those simmering hormones. No one was caught in the tower job, but everyone knew who had made the climb.

But then came that Monday when Corky appeared at school with a chunk of his thick ashy hair missing, and Alan, with an eye the color of a chemical spill.

"Yeah, we got into it Saturday night," Corky said. "That son of a bitch even tried to bite me."

Alan had no comment, nor did we learn what the fight was about. I'm sure that after eighteen or nineteen Big M's, they couldn't tell us either.

It's not that any of us completely trusted Corky, but at least we could see his wildness approaching and could follow it for miles in a certain direction. He'd include you in it if you wanted, and I'm just glad I made it home from that Emerson, Lake, and Palmer concert he drove us to in Tuscaloosa back in eleventh grade.

Until that freezing football night, though, Alan never invited me anywhere, and until I accepted that particular invitation, I never dreamed nor thought I would have gone with him anywhere. Was I the first person he invited that night? Would I feel better knowing I was? Would anyone else have jumped at the chance to go with him that night, or to follow him ever down his particular path?

Did anyone of good standing ever think to include him on theirs—to make him feel a part of something else, something more? I ask this, of course, futilely and much too late.

I think about the night we spent together in vast Legion Field more than I ever suspected I would. Maybe because it reminds me so much of the outings my own parents might have proposed: wholesome fun when I was nine or ten at a high school game with a stop for a late breakfast afterwards. Family night at the K-Mart in nearby Midfield, where I'd be as happy as I ever was, shopping for new 45's or being treated to a fountain Coke at the grill.

Maybe because I'm a fan of simple pleasures, of familial love.

I believe that Alan's parents loved him and loved the idea that I agreed to go with him. They knew my family. Like the Crosbys if you didn't really know them, we seemed so solid. Maybe they believed I would be a good influence on Alan. Maybe they believed that on this night they could relax a bit, enjoy a night like they had dreamed of having all those years before, back when they adopted him.

Maybe they believed that on this night their family had reached a turning point, a point even Alan could appreciate.

Maybe they felt better that night than they had in years and hoped this feeling of relaxation and safety and love would continue.

Maybe, as they drifted off to sleep that night, they were able to cast out of their minds the scene of their son and his guest sitting as far away from them as possible; of the sickly sweet smell on the two teenagers when they returned.

And maybe, nestled soundly in their warm bed, they didn't hear the back door softly open and close later that night when Alan stole into the woods and got "really fucked up," as he reported to me the following Monday.

"That old bastard and stupid bitch never knew," he said.

Alan transferred in our junior year to Bessemer Academy, one of the segregationist private schools so dear to certain white people in the early 70's. I'd run into him occasionally at Pasquale's Pizza or CT's Game Room, hangouts for our generation of Bessemer teens and stirring grounds for later festivities in cars, or the woods, or your own bedroom if, like Alan, your parents never checked on you to see what you were up to.

Mainly, though, I lost sight of Alan then, not that it bothered me. Life went on with Ray-Ray or Corky or Jimmy—guys whose mouths were always closed even if their eyes were only sometimes clear.

Hardly any of us went to the same college when that time came. Ray-Ray and I went to similar, small liberal arts schools, while most others chose either Alabama or Auburn. I don't remember where Alan went—likely to Bessemer Tech or Jeff State, junior colleges with lax standards. It seemed that somewhere during this time he got a job at the local country radio station doing something behind the aural scenes, something no one knew about or cared to verify.

The sad fact is that by this time, the mere words spoken by an unfortunate citizen, "I ran into Alan Crosby today," would cause otherwise confident and secure listeners to sigh or shake their heads or wince and emit audible moans, so clearly could they empathize with the poor speaker. So relieved were they that it wasn't they who had been run into and had to listen to unbelievable tales of drunken folly, or lies told too many times before.

So relieved they didn't have to invent their own lies just to escape him.

During those years I heard he was still living with his parents. By then, he had wrecked so many cars, had wrecked so many parts of himself, that he had to wear a colostomy bag. Someone even told me that Alan had become a "Narc." I never knew whether that was true.

I do know that even at the end, he still referred to his folks as "that dumb bastard" and "stupid bitch."

Psychologists will have us wonder about Alan. What was really wrong there, organic or artificial, nature or nurture? Did his so-called friends contribute to his disease by egging him on, believing him when we shouldn't have, encouraging him for our own entertainment so that we could sit around later without him and talk about what a "mad, crazy fucker" he was and that we wished he'd take his dumb ass and go away somewhere and leave us the fuck alone?

The last time I saw Alan was on a September Saturday in the early 1980's. My graduate school, being on the quarter system, didn't start until later in the month, which gave me a few extra weeks to enjoy my parents and watch an Alabama football game or two with my friends.

On this Saturday, Corky's older brother Dave and I are running errands in preparation for the game that we'll be attending with his wife and some other friends. We're at the 4th Avenue car wash, sprucing up his wife's Camaro. As Dave finishes wiping the front windshield, a slightly battered but over-revving Malibu pulls in.

"Oh shit," Dave says. "It's Alan Crosby."

He kind of sidles out of the car and lopes up, greeting us as if one of us has just returned from some foreign war. He's a sight: squirrelly-looking with red and half-lidded eyes, hair still wedgy and thick. Talking his talk about how fucked up he is and never noticing that we keep shifting backwards until we're up against the car.

And then he says "Hey, you guys watching the game later? Can I come over? I gotta get away from that old bastard."

"No man, Joyce's parents got us tickets to the game. In fact, we need to leave soon."

"Wow, do ya have an extra seat?"

"Sorry man. All we have is for us."

"All right. Maybe I'll call ya later. I got some good stuff."

We both say "Sure man," and then climb into Dave's car, taking wrong turns until we're out of sight and can head over to Dave's place where we'll gather with our friends and head to jam-packed Legion Field to watch Alabama lackadaisically defeat Georgia Tech.

"You don't think he'll call, do you," I ask Dave.

"Man, I hope not," Dave replies, and then we forget about Alan who never calls or bothers us again.

A year or so later, as I'm talking to my mother back home, she tells me that a few days before, Mrs. Crosby found Alan in his bedroom.

"They say it was an overdose. He was already blue."

I don't know if I ever heard, but most people concluded that it wasn't an accident. And maybe they're right. How would I know really? I did my best not to know what went on with Alan, the trouble he could bring. The trouble he knew.

"His poor mother," my mother said. "All the things she did for him and all the trouble he gave her."

They might have carved that sentiment on Alan's tombstone, but then, that's something else I'll never know since I didn't attend his funeral; since, even now as I write this some thirty years later, I still don't know where that boy whom I sat with for three intensely cold hours one long ago night is even buried.

17
"Hey, Did You Happen to See?"

I remember the day that AM radio first called me to life. It was June 1968, and I was eleven years old. The song I remember best on that day was The Temptations' "I Wish It Would Rain." Birmingham's WSGN must have played it three times that afternoon. It was an especially tough year to be living in Birmingham: I knew people who laughed when Dr. King was killed and who called Bobby Kennedy a "nigger-lover" even after Sirhan-Sirhan murdered him in a service area. The kids who laughed and rejoiced weren't inherently ignorant, poor, or trashy. But they were hard on anyone who was shy or plain, anyone whose skin color was dark, anyone who didn't fit into the crowd. It was difficult and usually impossible to buck these kids, that is, if you wanted to be part of the most popular group around.

On Facebook today, these no-longer kids are the ones "liking" the "Duck Dynasty" family. I can't lie. What they say still matters to me.

But one of the great equalizers in our youthful era was the AM radio. In Birmingham, that meant WSGN, WVOK, and WAQY. These stations, contrary to other public institutions in Birmingham, knew no racial bias, at least not in their playlists.

Neither did they discriminate among popular genres, playing healthy doses of Rock, Pop, Soul, R&B, and Country from Led Zeppelin to Marvin Gaye to Ray Price. Even the semi-classical theme from *Love Story* and Judy Collins' version of "Amazing Grace" made it to mainstream Birmingham airwaves. And if no one in my crowd admitted to loving Judy or Marvin, or Lynn Anderson's "I Never Promised You A Rose Garden," then explain to me why these songs lingered in the Top Ten week after week?

Hardly a day goes by when I'm not reminded of this era. I pass a fast food drive-in or sit in some carpool line; sometimes I'm even walking through the Prague airport and hear a piece of music I subjected my parents to. Or I read something about my culture, as I did last night when I picked up the latest issue of *The Oxford American* and ran across a beautiful, insightful journey into the history and fandom of Country star Charlie Rich. While the article should be required reading for anyone who cares about the 60's, or the South, or rawboned music, what hit me was the first page, the lyrics to Rich's most beloved song: "Hey, did you happen to see the most beautiful girl in the world?"

Why do song lyrics, or just those words on a page, make me travel to certain streets—to houses that I saw frequently but never entered? Why, when I hear Rich singing those words, do I remember a girl I barely knew from my high school days?

The music from that era is one thing. The era itself, quite another. I can't say that I was happy living then, happy that I *was* living then. For so many reasons I didn't fit: my long hair, my father who in the land of the protestants was Jewish, my refusal to hate Black people. But in one area at least, I was horribly normal, breathtakingly average.

In elementary school, I didn't understand what being class-conscious meant. What I knew was that some kids couldn't afford to bring lunch money or wear heavy coats in winter. That some kids smelled bad or didn't wear underwear and had to walk to school no matter the weather. My parents explained that some of these kids were so unfortunate that they didn't get to eat breakfast or might not have a parent waiting for them when they got home. That possibly their mothers or their daddies had left home years before, or were still there but drank excessively.

Once, my mother showed me a newspaper photograph of the mother of one of my second grade classmates. She had left her home, been arrested for some form of theft, and sent off to the women's prison near Montgomery.

"She's crazy," my mother said. "She just left those kids!"

And all three of her children were in my second grade class: a pair of twins who had been held back in first grade and their younger sister.

I knew these kids, knew they were poor, though I couldn't have told you why. I asked them, once, where they lived.

"Down Arlington. In the projects," the younger one said.

In one of the parts of our town that wasn't segregated, though not by anyone's choice.

They don't teach economics in second grade, but it was enough to see how many of the poorer kids struggled with basic reading and arithmetic. Many of my friends called these kids "dumb," said they had "cooties," and laughed at them often to their face.

And sometimes I did too. For I was privileged: a middle class boy with two parents who worked, cooked, and provided everything I needed, and often even what I wanted.

But in the supposed great equalizer of public school, middle-class kids like me got exposed to other kids who truly were left behind or who commonly used words like "bitch" or "bastard" or "nooky." I'm sure I would have learned these words anyway, but the fact is that I learned them in 1966 from kids who lived in broken down houses—kids who saw or experienced a world I was blessedly insulated from.

So in time, I became aware that "poor" meant low class,

crude, and trashy. "Poor white trash." That was the phrase we used. It followed me throughout high school, as I saw and judged kids who weren't exactly poor and certainly not trashy, but who lived in parts of town that were a step or two down from my neighborhood in the south hills of town where some of the earliest town pillars formerly dwelled before they moved to the exclusive Lakewood community just west of town. I knew these poorer kids were off limits as friends. I shouldn't want to play or ride with them, and certainly I shouldn't invite them to my house or set foot in theirs.

And as I moved through puberty, I knew that I could never think of dating anyone from such straitened places.

In my junior high days, I aspired to the highest of social cliques. But the closest I could get was to hover near these kids. I'd occasionally be invited to the right parties or have one of the cool guys over to spend the night with me. And even when I officially made it into the clique—though how I made it or why or even exactly when, I don't know—I still couldn't find a girlfriend within this crowd. I'd write notes and call and ask these girls out. They'd talk to me, sometimes for hours on the phone. But if I ever hinted at a date, they'd shut me down:

"Sorry, Momma's calling me."

"Don't you know that I like Don?"

"I'm not allowed to date someone who doesn't go to my church."

These were only the tips of my rejected iceberg.

Yet despite my frustrations and "striking out," I never considered asking out a girl who was "beneath" my social class. If I thought about it, I'd hear Johnny Rivers singing "The Poor Side of Town," and then I'd look again to the goddesses of my class—the Mary Jane's or Melissa's or Robyn's—and my fantasies would evaporate into the reality that if I asked out a girl who wasn't quite in my economic class, I'd be ridiculed or worse:

I might be considered one of them.

Today I see that some of the girls I liked in that highest clique were not so well off either. Their houses were small and plain, though clean and set in "acceptable" neighborhoods. Acceptable, at least, by the lower middle class standards of our insular community. I really don't know how I judged these things back then other than I listened to too many class-conscious people who passed their judgments on to me.

Judgments that kept me from seeing the most beautiful girl in that particular time and world: the one who sat right behind me in homeroom every day.

Karen was tall. "Lissome" is the word I'd use now. Golden brown hair hanging to her shoulders and in some years even longer. Her eyes were brown and set fairly wide apart. She used a heavier black eye shadow than most girls of that era, or at least most girls who moved in my circles. Her mouth was wide too, but it was hard to care because her lips were so full—not red exactly. In fact, I remember them as pale pink, and I don't remember her wearing lipstick or even gloss. Some of my friends said Karen had a Chinese look, though as far as I know, her parents were Caucasian.

I never met her parents; never saw them even once. Somehow though, I knew her father was gone, though I didn't know whether he had died or just left them. She had a sister, Debbie, two years older, equally tall with darker hair. Debbie epitomized the term "hippie chick" for me, especially when I spied her at the local mall, tooling down the corridors in bell-bottom jeans, brown moccasins, and beads dangling from her neck. I might not be remembering this correctly, but I think Debbie got pregnant early in life, not long after or perhaps even before she graduated high school. I knew that wasn't supposed to happen to kids in my group, though some time after I graduated, I realized that a couple of the supposedly "better" kids got a little too close in our junior year: one of those situations where the girl wears oversize coats for a couple of weeks, then one Monday, she looks just like her old self. Her old coatless self. And she remained in the popular group. If anyone in the group knew then, they just looked the other way—the way that all of that class can look because, of course, their class allows it. Funds it.

But Debbie chose otherwise. Or maybe she had no choice at all.

Karen's house sat on one of our main routes to the mall, at the intersection of Clarendon and Ninth Street, a neighborhood that middle class people escaped once their incomes said they could. If you looked to the left before you turned onto Ninth, you'd see it, second from the corner, on the opposite side of the street. Two rocking chairs sat on the front porch, and in all seasons, one or both of the sisters would be rocking in them, talking, looking out to the street, thinking about guys or music, or something I'll never know that went on in the world within their house.

In our alphabetically ordered high school homeroom, Karen sat next to Mary Kate Blake who had bleached-blond hair set in a semi-beehive. I don't believe they were just desk-friends, for I could hear them discussing more than homework on those occasions that my own desk-mate, Gary Barlow, wasn't trying to talk to me. I'd be lying if I said I could recount anything Karen or Mary Kate said after all these years. But I'd guess that their boyfriends were often in the mix. I don't know who Mary Kate liked, but for some of these years, Karen liked an "older" boy, Ricky Russo, whom I'd had seen around since first grade. He was one grade above us, and as far as I know, was a nice enough guy.

Once, I intruded on Karen and Mary Kate's talk, informing them that the football game that week was being played not at home, but in Oxford. "My Dad's driving some of us," I said, and as I looked into their faces, or more correctly, into Karen's face, I know a part of me hoped she'd say, "Oh...could I have a ride?" But of course she didn't. As marginally in that upper clique as I was, Karen knew that my world and hers would never get any closer than that three feet of desk separating her chair from mine.

I know she knew this. I knew this.

But I never considered that she might have hoped otherwise; I can only wonder now if she ever did.

That's how life went back then. Eventually I dated four or five different girls in my high school years; some I brought home to meet my parents, others, I didn't. Whenever I did get a date, though, it wasn't my parents' approval I sought, at least not at first.

My first date was with a Baptist girl, which is only significant because in the years before I started dating, my mother issued this warning:

"You can date anyone you want to, just so long as she's not a Baptist."

She never fully explained that warning except to add that, "Baptists are funny," and not in the Ha-Ha way.

But when it came to my friends, I always tried to pick girls that met their approval. Or stay away from those who didn't. I can't believe it now, but I know I did.

Or maybe I should admit that I believe it now all-too-well.

Some time after we graduated, my best high school friend Ray-Ray confessed that he found Karen to be exotically attractive. Ray-Ray had come out of the closet by then, but in high school could have had any girl he wanted. Most of the girls he wanted—and many that he got—were also the ones I wanted, but never got. So if he had told me in tenth grade that he thought Karen was worth going after, maybe I would have considered talking to her.

Maybe.

It was only when I got to college that I realized that the "in group" I tried so hard to belong to wasn't worth it—that they were, in the end, that era's high school snobs. And it was only then that I realized who Karen was: a girl I snubbed; a girl I couldn't appreciate.

A girl who never looked down on me.

The C-Shell Lounge, circa 1975. I've just finished my freshman year in college, and my roommate and I are having beers to celebrate. He's from my hometown: Rodney Rockett, a guy I've known since kindergarten though we didn't become good friends until we were thrown together as dorm mates.

The C-Shell Lounge is the bar in Bessemer's Ramada Inn—one of the few places in Bessemer where you can get draft beer and dance—named after its proprietor, Claude Shell, a 70-year old man whose "assistant" was a 30-ish woman named Phoebe.

I've often wondered what it must feel like to name a Ramada Inn lounge after yourself.

The lounge itself is dark with swiveling black faux leather chairs and a murky-colored shag carpet, perhaps reminiscent of a beach bar somewhere. I'll know the C-Shell better next summer when I become the part-time handy-man at the motel, which means that every Sunday morning I'll get to clean the bar and cart twenty-five enormous garbage bags full of Pabst and Bud bottles to the dumpster. Not to mention all the plastic cups and cigarette butts. All for minimum wage, which in the summer of 1976 is $2.25 an hour. My earnings go toward helping pay for one semester's tuition and room/board at The University of Montevallo, which is the self-proclaimed "best bargain in higher education" in Alabama. I would have rather gone to Birmingham-Southern or "Sewanee" with my best friends, but tuition in those institutions is three times what I'm paying, and there just aren't enough Sunday morning beer cans in the C-Shell Lounge.

So Rodney and I are sipping our Buds and feeding the jukebox, which contains a sordid combination of rock/pop and country and all points in between. Elton John's "Don't Let the Sun Go Down On Me" has just finished, and true to his name, Rodney has also punched in "Rocket-Man," and he sings along as if the song was written for him. About that moment I look up and see two girls I know enter the bar: Susan, who lives just down the street from me, and Karen.

They sit at a table near us, and then Susan calls my name.

Though we've known each other since 7th grade, we're the sort of acquaintances who will always speak to each other, maybe exchange neighborhood gossip, but that's usually it.

They move to the table next to ours. Susan and I talk, and every time I glance over at Karen, she looks down. Is she shy? Ashamed? I don't know, but she's wearing flared-brown jeans and a loose top with sleeves hanging to her wrists. Her hair is longer now too, straight and lush. So far, we haven't said a word.

An upbeat song pours from the jukebox: "Let Your Love Flow" by The Bellamy Brothers. This is their one pop hit, for afterward they will declare for the Country side of things and I will forget that they ever made the pop charts, except when I recall this scene: the definite beat, the precious melody. The moment when I ask Karen to dance.

She finally looks at me and says,

"To that?"

"Well, it's not that bad. Besides, it's just dancing."

I don't know what makes me say any of this, what I'm thinking other than there's music, a dance floor, a girl who's pretty beyond reason sitting next to me. She takes my hand and we move to the dance floor, joining two or three other couples. I'm used to dancing at urban clubs where a more pulsating early Disco beat from Van McCoy or Silver Convention prescribes all moves. "Let Your Love Flow," however, seems to beg a beat, to insist that you put one foot here, another there as if you wouldn't know what to do otherwise. Also, it's not a sexy song: "Let your love flow, like a mountain breeze, and let your love flow to all living things." Maybe this is what Karen questioned when I asked her to dance. But she's game, and we're both trying to hit that perfect beat and not look stupid doing it. I don't know what music she's used to dancing to, and I don't know what she's looking for in this bar with its seedy furnishings. And honestly, I don't know what I'm looking for either.

After the song, we return to our table, and the four of us talk. Both girls have been living at home this year, working temporary jobs in retail. Rodney tells them about his communications courses, that he'd like to get into TV production.

"I'm planning to major in Social Work so that I can help the disadvantaged and downtrodden."

And I actually used those words. It wasn't like the girls' eyes glazed over when I spoke, but something happened. Something vacant and disinterested. Or maybe something worse.

Each of us ordered another round of beers. The music got even more predictable. The last song I remember was by another pop band, Exile. Their hit was a love song underlain with a pseudo-disco thump: "Kiss You All Over." They, too, would later abandon pop for country. So strange.

We didn't dance to this song, but when it ended, almost by mutual consent, we all decided it was time to go. There was still a lot of night left in our summertime.

But in that time, we were all still living at home. With our parents.

I've told myself until now that it was that reality that stopped me from pursuing anything with Karen.

Home.

But hearing those old songs, seeing Charlie's lyrics now after all these years: I know it was actually the held-over stigma from the preceding years of actually getting closer to a girl who wasn't part of "the crowd" I normally hung with. Even though there was none of my former crowd around.

Even though I had just spent a couple of hours in a lounge named for a man who was living some sort of playboy dream.

So in the parking lot of the C-Shell Lounge out near the Bessemer Super Highway, I watched Karen get in Susan's car and drive away, maybe to her home, or maybe to another seedy club where the night was still as young as she needed it to be.

I went home too, and though I can't say that I kept thinking about her as I lay in bed that night and the ones after, I didn't exactly forget her either. Bob Dylan might have chastised me that "I threw it all away," that night, but he wouldn't be right except in the way that I couldn't see then beyond the hills of my own class. I couldn't see then, as I do now, that class isn't an illusion.

Five years after high school, a few grads think it's a grand idea to reunite the senior high class of 1974. They rent a party hall at the Ramada Inn. The same one where I worked three summers earlier, emptying beer bottles and checking the pool for chlorine levels, and on occasion, moving a bad TV out of a room and swapping it for a marginally better one so that the poor tenant could choose from Rockford or Magnum and then give me a barbecue sandwich as a tip. He had gotten two by mistake from Pike's Barbecue just down the road. I took the sandwich but told him that Bob Sykes' Barbecue was better.

The C-Shell Lounge, for some reason, was off-limits to we former seniors. So we crammed into a party room about the same size as a double classroom from our high school days.

Apropos of the strained integration of those high school years, the white alums sat in one half of the room, the Black grads in the other. There was a middle aisle where occasional mixed ex-students gathered. I stood there for a while talking to senior class president Henry Scott, and later to Coach Moton who was maybe supposed to be chaperoning, or maybe just wanted to relive the good times. He was a fair-minded man who once found my stolen gym socks and got them back for me. I wondered back then what sort of a person stole sweaty gym socks. But Coach Moton seemed to know quite well. I don't think they could have possibly paid him enough back then, even though he was assistant head coach, imported from the now-closed all-Black high school.

Eventually, he got the head-coaching job, but by then, most of the white families had pulled out of the Bessemer public system.

But on this night, like the rest of us, he watched all that hadn't really changed in our lives. Most of the white guys in my former in-group wore white oxford-cloth shirts and khakis. Their wives looked matronly already. Some had been married since graduation; others were even divorced.

I was still single and heading off to graduate school that coming fall. I wore a pair of un-dyed Levis that Ray-Ray, who considered reunions a form of intestinal disorder, sent me from New York. They looked sharp with my black boots, or at least I thought they did. My hair was frighteningly long for Bessemer, even in 1979. It's true that I felt and looked different from my peers. It's also true that part of me still wanted to fit in.

The music was a DJ playing tunes from our high school era mixed with newer bands like Bad Company and Heart. At some point, the soul of Al Green and Earth, Wind, and Fire morphed into disco, and I might be crazy, but I think the DJ even played "Rapper's Delight."

I remember dancing with my friend Jim's wife for a while, and then catching up with Jo Beth, a girl I sort of dated back when Todd Rundgren sang "Hello It's Me."

About an hour or so into the night, as I was wondering how long I'd really stay at this event, Karen walked in. She was dressed in a plain gray skirt, sleeved blouse, and matching gray pumps. She came by herself, carrying an umbrella, for the summer rain was coming down and it wasn't so gentle.

I watched her look around, walk to a semi-occupied table, and place her umbrella against it. She stood there looking beautiful.

She stood there looking at me.

So I got up and walked over to her. She smiled, and so did I. There wasn't much to say, and if there was, I certainly didn't say it.

I keep thinking now of that episode of "The Andy Griffith Show" where Andy's high school flame returns for their reunion. Barney calls theirs the most "natural romance" of any couple in their class. Well, Karen and I weren't natural anythings.

But I asked her if she'd like something to drink, and she said yes.

We stood there acknowledging all the other couples, the kids she never knew well; the ones I knew better than I could say.

I didn't know what had happened in the four years since I saw her just a few hundred yards away at the C-Shell Lounge on the night she rode away with Susan. But it felt like a lifetime of college had never occurred for me. It felt like I had left her just the night before.

The dance floor was remarkably alive, and as we wondered what would play next, I recognized the opening bars of a song from that senior year—one that played all the time on our AM stations but that none of us much acknowledged.

For it simply wasn't cool to say you liked, or in my case loved, Charlie Rich's "Behind Closed Doors."

"My baby makes me smile, Lord don't she make me smile..."

I didn't have to ask Karen this time. We just walked to the dance floor and held each other for the next three-and-a-half minutes.

When the song ended, she looked at me and said,

"I have to go; I'm leaving town tomorrow."

"Really, why?"

"Because I'm joining the Air Force."

"Oh."

I stared at her a minute, thinking that whatever I'd expected to happen, this wasn't it. But I also surprised myself. I accepted her reality, something that was maybe her dream and certainly her way out of this world, this "Bessemer." In that moment I was happy for her. She seemed happy at least, and more than that, she seemed brave. In that moment, she outclassed everyone at the dance.

"Well, I'll walk out with you."

So she put on her coat, took up her umbrella, and without saying goodbye to anyone else, we walked out the door to her car. Standing there in the light of the Ramada Inn sign, I leaned over and kissed her. We parted once, kissed again, and then she said calmly,

"I better go."

"Really?"

"Yes. Because if I don't leave now I..."

She slowly pulled away from me. I watched her as she left the inn. As she left my life.

I left then too, and though I went to other reunions, Karen was never there.

I've been married for thirty years to the woman I was supposed to marry, someone of whom most of my old Bessemer friends would have never approved, much less understood. We married on a summer day, June 21st, the longest day of the year. My wife is from Iran, but I didn't marry her in consideration or in spite of those old friends. That much, at least, I learned from Karen. To my face, one of my old friends once slurred my wife's background. That's the dark side of Bessemer, and I'm sure there are even darker spots—spots that I now believe Karen knew all-too-well. I wonder what it would have been like had I recognized back then that these "friends" weren't really that. I wonder what might have happened had I seen and known Karen and been friends with her. What did she feel or see back then? She chose her own way and didn't seem to care what anyone in our class thought about it. Or anyone I knew, at least.

Recently I learned that while in the Air Force, she met and married a commercial jet pilot. They travel the world together now and are reported to be quite happy.

Life truly is a revolving door. Just this evening, visiting my old hometown, I decide to drive by the brick house where Karen used to live. I know the house when I see it. And for a second, I think I see two rocking chairs there on the front porch as I approach. But that isn't true after all. Instead, there is an aluminum barbecue pit and a folding chair. Otherwise, the house looks just as I remember it. I wonder who's living there now. It looks like a good place to live, just as it always has.

I hope it was a good place for Karen, but as with so many other things, I'll never really know what went on behind those doors, in a world that I finally see was not so far from mine.

18
Racial Divide

In the summer of 1989, my wife and I traveled to Bessemer to celebrate my birthday with my parents who had clandestinely orchestrated a gathering of some of my long-lost childhood friends. I should have noticed how carefully my mother had cleaned and redecorated our den. That comfortable room with its cushy sofa, laz-y-boy recliner, and console stereo had hosted past teen parties celebrating my seventeenth birthday and my high school graduation. Now its warm yellow, blue, and orange-colored décor was arranged to welcome this more grown-up occasion—my adult friends, ready to honor and celebrate the man I had become: the man who left home and brought the world back with him.

On the morning after our arrival, I rose at 6:00 am, a habit I had gotten into ever since my wife's pregnancy had begun causing her extreme nausea. This was our first child, and I had adapted to the morning regime of bananas, applesauce, soft-boiled eggs—anything my wife could keep down, if only for thirty minutes. On some evenings I sautéed liver and onions to combat her anemia, holding my own bile the entire time. Turned out, she adored liver. Such are the mysteries of a pregnant woman's cravings.

But on this morning as I was gathering her tray, the phone rang. My old-world Southern mother often receives calls before eight am. So I thought nothing of this one until I heard her musical soprano drop an octave.

"Oh, I see...yes, he's right here."

I took the receiver though I really didn't want to. It was my wife's sister.

"Terry, Baba-Jun passed away last night. I didn't want to call you then because I knew you'd be so tired, and Nilly needed her sleep. I know it's your birthday, too, and I hate to do this, but like my husband said, you'll have plenty of others."

"Baba-Jun," in Farsi, translates to "Dear Father." My wife is Persian, an immigrant from Iran. Her entire family arrived in the US in ripples between 1979 and 1984.

My mind flooded at this point. Naturally, my primary concern was my Iranian wife who was currently lying in my childhood bed in the house in which both my mother and I had grown up. But my parents had been counting on this visit for months. Now what? They used to claim that I chose girlfriends based on how far I'd have to drive *their* car to see them. Could they have conceived in those simpler days that I would travel the lengths of the earth for love? Was there ever a distance too far for me?

But sometimes the world, or in this case a gorgeous Middle Eastern girl, comes calling.

Since my marriage, I know that my parents had often felt cheated by how much time and energy I had invested in my wife's family. Here, then, was another interruption, albeit one that we all lamented in our various worlds.

My bedroom was two rooms away from the phone. I tried to keep my voice low as I spoke to my sister-in-law. I wanted to break the news to my wife as gently as possible, but when I walked into the bedroom, her piercing, raven-black eyes, now moist and fearful, told me that she had already heard it all.

Every weekend before this one, we had traveled from our home in upstate South Carolina to Knoxville to visit her father whom we all knew was dying of prostate cancer. While in Iran, he had been falsely imprisoned by the Ayatollahs, during which time he suffered a major heart attack. Upon his release, his prostate condition went unchecked for too long. He could have survived had he received proper and timely treatment. He was only sixty-four.

I held my wife as she cried, whispering words of love for her and for her Baba.

My mother entered a few minutes later and together she and my wife shocked me with news about my surprise party.

"My God! I can't believe you kept this a secret from me and for so long! No one ever surprises me."

"You'll have to call everyone now and tell them what happened," Mom said.

"Don't worry about that. Of course everyone will understand."

Then they gave me my present: a first edition of *Joyce's Finnegans Wake*, the irony of its title lost on everyone but me.

I was moved beyond sound: they didn't understand a word of the precious book they bought me, and if they knew of its deeper absurdities, they might wonder why anyone would want it or pay so much money for it. To me, though, it was my greatest literary treasure: a novel without a clear beginning or ending. A dream. Or maybe a nightmare, given the strange association it would now have for me.

I hugged my mother, kissed my wife who was so happy for me despite her own grief.

Later, my mother presented me with the guest list: my old friend Fred! Hadn't seen him since his wedding eight years ago. There were a few others I'd regret not seeing too, but as I scanned the list, I saw two names that I would have certainly banned had I been consulted.

Robert, Amy, and I had spent countless hours as far back as junior high going to parties, church outings, Marshall Tucker

Band concerts, and various other non-sanctioned events. Over one long summer in the early 1980's, as we wasted both time and ourselves tossing a Frisbee in random country meadows, I watched these two grow closer. And so at the end of that August, I wasn't a bit surprised when they announced their engagement. I was in their wedding and was naturally part of the entourage they invited to a weekend mountain cabin afterward to further celebrate their joy.

The mountain cabin they rented for this group honeymoon comfortably housed the twelve of us who gathered on that October weekend. Robert grilled steaks for everyone that first night, and couples were seated four to a table with candlelight and wine. It felt so adult, so warm, like we would all be friends forever even though most of us had already moved states away. My girlfriend at the time seemed to fit in with everyone, though when I look back at it now, fitting in meant tossing a Frisbee with a straight arm, rolling a perfect joint, and being willing to stay up all night playing card games while listening to 70's rock. Maybe that's why she and I broke up a few weeks later.

"I really wish you hadn't invited them," I said to my mother. "Now I've got to call."

"Why, what's the matter?"

But we needed to get on the road to Knoxville soon, and I had neither the time, nor the patience to explain.

So I began dialing.

II

Four years earlier, I came home because I had gotten married in secret, and it was time to tell my parents. To say that I felt guilty would be like saying that I loved Southern hickory-smoked barbecue. My parents, of course, *knew* my wife; we had been to visit on several occasions, and they liked her. They just didn't know that a year earlier, she had actually *become* my wife.

I remember standing in the den of my parents' home, scene of years of family evenings gathered there in front of an ongoing series of black and white and then color Motorolas. The one behind me now was wrapping up the national news. Reagan's face filled the screen as he mouthed the mindless platitudes that marked his reign—platitudes my father clung to as if they had come straight from the Torah. My parents were doing the evening dishes in the kitchen that adjoined the den via an eight-foot wide rectangular "window." My father could therefore dry each dish while viewing his favorite programs.

For several long moments the three of us stood on opposite sides of that window, staring at what we couldn't understand.

"Where did we go wrong?" my father asked.

"Wrong? What do you mean 'wrong?' You've done everything right! Nilly and I love each other. She's kind, generous, and I'd trust her with my life. What else should I want?"

Dad shrugged, placed the final dinner plate in the cabinet, and turned to my mother who remained eerily silent.

"I don't know. I just don't know."

They didn't ask why we had been so secretive, why we didn't allow them into our trust. Maybe they knew, as I did, that had I discussed the plan with them beforehand, or asked their blessing, they would have resisted and tried to talk me out of it. They would have expressed their doubts and fears of my marrying outside my culture. Outside of the two "faiths" that they, in their own married rebellion, had brought together and that so loosely joined our family.

In the early 1950s when they married, neither side of my parents' family welcomed their union. My mother's mother, a righteous Protestant matriarch, was dismayed that her daughter had chosen a Jewish man seven years her senior—a man who still

lived in his own parents' home. My father's mother, a demanding vessel dispensing guilt and shame in equal proportions, refused to attend their ceremony unless a rabbi officiated. No rabbi within thirty miles would do so, however, because my parents confessed that they would raise their children in my mother's faith.

I imagine the distance they felt, that awful divide, sitting across my father's rabbi's desk. The stern refusal; the embarrassed silence.

Finally, a Montgomery, Alabama, rabbi agreed to unite them. He drove 200 miles round trip in one afternoon to do so and made fifty dollars for his services.

Rabbi Blachschleger.

Despite his good faith, my father's mother nevertheless sat shiva for her apostate son. He was now dead to her, though that didn't stop her from calling on him to flip her bed mattress monthly, as well as for other assorted chores, over the next forty years. A forty-year period when he drove his new family every Sunday without fail the twenty-mile trip over foothill back roads so that we could sit at the feet of this scornful woman.

And then we'd drive home again—to the house where he and my mother wed. The same house she grew up in and where we all lived with her mother, the house's legal owner.

Needless to say, my two grandmothers had issues that divided our family, issues left unspoken and so unresolved over the span of twenty years until my mother's mother died.

"I'm just afraid that one day they'll try to force you to move to Iran," my mother finally said.

At least her real objection was on the table.

"Don't worry about that, please. I'm not moving to Iran. What would I do there? For God's sake, they *had* to move *here*. They got political asylum. Nobody wants to move back there."

Which was true enough, although at that moment, my

mother-in-law was in Iran trying to secure some of their retirement funds that the government had seized. Originally, we had hoped to tell my parents when she returned so that we could stage the wedding that my mother had always dreamed for me. But the waiting was just too hard, compounding my guilt daily as if it were interest on my meager savings—guilt that I couldn't bear because my parents were practically the last ones to know. My new in-laws knew the truth from the start. They were behind our marriage from the very beginning and seemed to have fallen in love with me before my wife did.

"They liked you so much that I almost refused to keep seeing you," my wife confessed not long after our wedding. "I was only twenty-one. What did I know?"

My in-laws said to me, "You are our son!" At first, I was taken aback at these words. Would I now be theirs and theirs only? They were looking out for their daughter's best interests and knew, somehow, that we were right for each other: A true match.

It was like an arranged marriage, except that I was my own representative. I received my future in-laws' blessing, but what about the one from *my* parents?

So after our brief service at the Knoxville court house—a service actually performed in the maintenance shed behind the court house by a "dignitary" who no doubt used the five dollar fee he required of me for a nice bottle of syrupy-sweet wine—we returned to my in-laws' apartment. They had prepared the traditional Persian wedding dish—Shirin Polo—made of saffron rice with almonds, slivered orange peel, and baked chicken.

When I told my close friends of this joyous occasion, most of them found our news exciting and romantic. Such good friends!

For my parents, though, "exciting" and "romantic" clearly didn't express their view toward us. In their hour of lamentation for their first-born son, they camped in the kitchen while I soldiered on in the den, the distance between us decidedly unbridged.

Finally, because one side had to move, I asked:

"Will you at least talk to her now? You know how much she

cares about both of you, and she's pretty nervous about all of this."

A pause. Then…a shift.

"Yes. Get her on the phone. It's all done now anyway," my mother sighed.

III

In the Alabama of my childhood, bridging a great divide wasn't exactly an event to commemorate. In the 1960s and 70s, no one divided the state more than George Wallace did. If you were an ardent supporter of the "Battlin" Judge-turned Governor, as my friend Jamie and his family were, you were likely to shower any conversation with a liberal use of the epithet "Nigger," as in "Kennedy's just a nigger-lover," or "Don't drink from that fountain. It's for niggers." And it often got worse. When Black children passed down our street, Jamie, his Eagle-Scout older brother Bill, or even his Daddy would yell "Sic 'em" to "Blackie," their dog, and follow that command with "You better run nigger!"

Though I never joined in the shouting, once, I did get swept away in the excitement: "Dad-blame-it, they sure can run. Gosh!" Instantly, Jamie's mother turned to me and said: "That's vulgar, and we don't use slang around our house. You're taking God's name in vain."

I had no idea what she was talking about then. I barely understand now. Did she think I knew, at age five, that my words were substitutes for "God Damn" and "God?" Did she believe I understood her admonishments and my own offense? Did she truly believe that I was shrewd enough to hide a purposeful blasphemy?

Jamie's family and mine were all members of the same Methodist church. Though many of the church's teachings simply ran though the sieve of my consciousness, I did hear and believe this one: "Love thy neighbor as thyself." And, I realize now, I thought everyone else at my church believed it too. For we all sang "He Lives" on Easter Sunday and attended *Messiah* on the first Sunday afternoon of each December. But in the late 60's, when a Black family of four—daddy, mama, a little girl and boy—visited one

Sunday, Jamie's family led the charge that tried to fire the "nigger-loving" preacher who let them in.

My parents detested George Wallace, and they forbade my brother and me from using the word "nigger," telling us instead to say "colored" or "Negro." If they heard Jamie or any other friend say "nigger" in our house, they would order these children home. And if the friend lived too far to walk, I clearly remember Mama putting us all in the car and driving the offending boy to his parents' care. Part of me hated seeing my playmates go home; another part of me, maybe the bigger part, relaxed when they did.

Despite my folks' inoculations, I became infected by kids' talk. Once, after hearing a friend say "Bastard" at everything that angered him, I called my own brother one. I didn't count on his racing inside and informing our mother, verbatim, of my offense. But he did, and she proceeded to literally wash my mouth out with soap.

However, my mother didn't hear everything I said. One summer morning as our long-time family maid Dissie was straightening our bedroom and humming some unknown-to-us spiritual, my brother and I staged a puppet show. With my "Frances the Mule" and his "Mr. Ed," we had a good rendition of our act going. Out of nowhere and almost unconsciously, my puppet called my brother's puppet a "nigger." He stared at my silver puppet. I stared at his brown one. Then *our* eyes met. All in the silence of seconds.

Everything stood still before us, except for Dissie who kept on cleaning and straightening our lives and humming the tune that always managed to see her through her day.

She never said a word about my remark to anyone.

IV

"Well, I love you too."

My mother handed me the receiver, and I assured my Persian bride that all was well.

"I think the hardest part is over. Don't worry, they'll be fine," I said, perhaps more calmly than I really felt. "And anyway, Robert and Amy are coming over soon, and when I told them about us, they were cool. The rest of the night will be pretty light, I think."

We hung up then after whispering our "I love you's." I wished that I could hold her, that she was here with me, but we both realized my parents and I needed the privacy to say what we had to. Though it had been difficult, we all had survived the feelings of shock, secrecy, and betrayal. I never doubted that we would. For despite our past conflicts over hair length, car privileges, ragged flannel shirts, and extremely loud rock music, my parents and I trusted each other. While they imposed tight curfews and made me work during high school and college summers, they also allowed me room to grow and make choices. I chose my own college, my various majors. I refused to consider ROTC as a viable payment option for those college years. And when I was ready, I stopped attending the church that never truly was my choice.

My parents helped me stretch. They financed a high school trip to Europe, somehow. They insisted that I accept a patronage position with my congressman in DC, which meant dropping out of college for a term.

They helped open the gap of independence between us, and I think we all believed that it would never get so wide that we'd be unable to stretch across it and touch each other.

But with my wedding announcement, I also realized that when you stretch, you're likely to wrench a joint or two.

When Robert and Amy arrived, we cracked open our Budweisers, settled down on the velvety sofa in our den, and caught up as old friends do. My parents hung with us for an hour or so, and the troves of gossip kept us laughing and light. I love the lightness that sixteen ounces of beer provide. The loosening of tongues, the breakdown of anxious inhibitions. And when my folks excused themselves to get ready for bed, I welcomed the chance to totally let go with my pals.

Part of me wished that we had a concert to attend or were about to hit our favorite club for a night of dancing as we used to do every weekend in the not-so-distant past. If it were still daylight, I would have suggested that we head outdoors to fly my master-Frisbee one more time.

In hindsight, that's what we should have done.

Instead, we settled deeper into the cushions.

With Robert grinning by her side as if he knew exactly what she was about to ask, Amy, with her pixie haircut, merry eyes, and a laugh that for so many years never failed to charm me, leaned forward and said:

"So Terry, what's it like to be married to one of those 'sand-niggers?'"

And she and Robert chuckled as if we were all in on the joke.

Until Amy uttered it, I had never heard that phrase before, didn't know it existed. I had heard "camel jockey" applied to a fellow grad student's Iranian husband, but the speakers were only pseudo-tough guys observing a mixed couple waiting at a bus stop. They had no history with this couple—my grad school friends—making their remark racist, but impersonal. Which left me, upon hearing a slur far worse, exactly where?

I have no clear recollection today of the moment after the offense. They had been such good friends. How can I explain the depth of our friendship, what I thought we had?

This felt like the end of something, and even then I wasn't sure exactly what was ending. Later that night I called my oldest, best friend, a guy we all loved; a guy who had "come out" to all of us years earlier. I knew he'd understand what I was feeling:

"I'm sure she was just kidding," Ray-Ray appeased.

"Yes, I know she thought so," I said. "But how can Amy kid about this? How can I ever *not* hear those words when I see or think of her?"

"You can't," he sighed. "You just can't."

I realized then that I had stayed silent to the "niggers" of the past—all those times when I heard friends use that hateful word. It seemed so abstract then, so distant. We didn't have Black friends or really know any Black kids. Like it or not, in the world of my youth, my friends and I lived on the same side of something:

a divide that for too long I never had to cross.

And now, the side I had chosen to live on spoke a different language—a language that didn't contain this abhorrent word.

I felt glad in that moment that I was leaving Bessemer the next day. For the first time in my experience of leaving "home," I knew that I *wouldn't* be leaving a part of me behind.

That moment was coming, but in the one before me, where Amy and Robert grinned so expectantly, I stammered some self-deprecating words—words intended to defuse this horrible situation. Perhaps I'm totally wrong. It seems to me now, though, that in those awkward minutes, our den, the rectangular window leading to our kitchen, my parents' bedroom, all the rooms of our house, and all the phone lines between my old world in Alabama and my new one in South Carolina, went absolutely quiet.

Dead.

Maybe I told them that I was tired. Maybe I said that I had a long drive the following morning and needed some sleep. Maybe. In any case they left, and the three of us never spoke together again.

V

Since I had kept this scene, those dividing moments, to myself, I couldn't fairly explain to my family why I didn't want Amy and Robert attending my birthday party. I wasn't sure why they even accepted my mother's invitation.

So I called, not knowing how the conversation would go.

Robert answered the phone, sounding half-asleep, a normal condition for him although it was pretty early on a Saturday morning. After listening to me explain the state of affairs in our world—our loss, our sadness—he began his tale:

"Well, we probably weren't coming anyway. It's been hard lately. Amy and I might be breaking up."

He said that Amy was asleep upstairs and he didn't want to wake her.

"I'm really sorry for you," I said. "I hope things work out."

Which they did. Robert and Amy divorced later that year, and frankly, I didn't know how that made me feel.

On the five-hour drive to Knoxville that day, my wife told stories of her father, who had been an oil company executive. She told of the house he built for their family in an affluent Tehran suburb, of the vegetable garden he grew, of the American cars he loved— especially his Pontiac which he had transported from America to Europe and which he then drove from France all the way to Iran. And of the beach house on the Caspian Sea that the family visited several times a year, driving the three hours to get there through the snow-capped Alborz Mountains on hazardous roads with no side-rails. Of the beautiful white sand that my wife, her sisters, and cousins played in by the water, not many miles from that other mountain range that links the Caspian to the Black Sea: The Caucasus. Seeing her pictures of those days reminds me of my own family vacations at the Gulf of Mexico, the white sands of both beaches seemingly identical.

The sand on the Caspian shore was the only sand that my wife saw during her sixteen years living in Iran.

VI

There are secrets we can't wait to reveal and some we never will. My parents love my wife and our two daughters. They appreciate the good life we lead, the example we set in our community.

I never told any of them what happened with Robert and Amy. I just couldn't. I couldn't say that word again, a word used against me and the person I love most in the world.

A few years ago, on the occasion of my oldest friend Ray-Ray's fiftieth birthday party in Bessemer, I ran into Amy. We were very cordial. She had remarried, it turned out, but hadn't brought her new husband to the party. My wife hadn't accompanied me either, owing to our youngest daughter's soccer tournament.

"You go and have fun," she said. "Believe me, I'll be fine here."

At one point in the evening, as Amy was laughing with another friend, she turned toward me. When our eyes met, I searched them for a minute. Did she remember that night more than twenty years earlier? Did she ever think about those words? And did she wonder at the fact that I never called when I came to town? I saw none of the answers in her eyes, though, and soon she was laughing with yet another friend, remembering something else from the past.

Something more comfortable.

The next morning as I was power walking through my mother's neighborhood, I came to Robert's old house. Though his father still lives there, Robert, too, has since remarried and moved a few counties away. As I passed, I felt that strange sensation of what "used to be" in the days in which we had the comfort of believing we were all the same under our skin.

I thought of all of this again this past summer when I taught Sherman Alexie's *Indian Killer* to my freshman literature class. In it, a serial killer is plaguing Seattle, and many people believe he must be an Indian. White thugs hit the streets ready to massacre anyone with a reddish aura. As a gang corners one victim, they scream at him and call him a "Prairie Nigger." Without missing a beat, he responds by telling them that his people never lived on a prairie; they live by rivers. So to be accurate, he says they should call him "Salmon-Nigger." I read this section to my class, and before I knew it, I was recounting *my* story to them. I told it all, and they listened intently, the seven white kids and the one black student, as if we were all sitting not on hard plastic classroom chairs, but on comfortable sofas and laz-y-boys in the den of a loving family's home.

I don't know yet if it felt cathartic to unload this weighted tale from my past. My students' generation has already bridged gaps that irrevocably separated members of mine. As I looked into *their* blue, brown, and black eyes, I knew they understood.

And I knew then that it was time to tell my story to the ones I love.

19
Star-Crossed

The cross fixed to the water tower high above my house is blazing red now. I've never seen it red before, so I ask:

"Momma, why has the cross turned red?"

"It's because someone's died in a wreck tonight. The police use the red signal to let us know."

We live in the section of town called South Highlands, on the side of a sloping neighborhood of comfortable houses. The water tower sits on Holbrook Avenue, two streets above ours. As we take our nightly walks, I look for certain comforting signs: The oak tree at the end of our block; the cars parked up and down our street in their accustomed driveways; and the cross. The pure, bright, white-lighted cross which, to me, is another of the thousands of luminous stars scattered across our night sky, keeping watch over my family.

I had always felt so safe in its presence. But I never wondered before this night exactly what it meant, and why it was there.

On the next night and for all the ones after, the cross will be white again. Or maybe I just stopped noticing it after that year—the year I turned five. But after that red night, I have always noticed something else:

Crosses mean danger.

❦

When I saw the tiny gold cross hanging off my nineteen-year old daughter Pari's olive-toned neck, I wondered where I had gone wrong. It's true that as a Jew, I get itchy at the sight of a cross. I always have, even though I haven't always been a Jew. In the days when I was nominally a Christian, the eight-foot cross hanging high above the altar in our Methodist church mesmerized me, like I was staring at a King Cobra doing its dance of poisonous death. Even without Jesus nailed on it, I could still see him clearly, sagging with a weight I couldn't comprehend due to the supposed "goodness" of this sacred sacrifice. I love ghost stories and the supernatural, and though macabre tales can scare me, I never take them personally. Staring at my church's cross, I knew that I was supposed to take the execution and rebirth of Jesus personally, but I just couldn't.

I was a Christian for the first twenty years of my life—a christened member of my mother's church. For the fifteen years after that, I was agnostic. For the last twenty years I've been a Jew, attending my father's temple in Birmingham whenever I visit home. In upstate South Carolina where I've lived over this Jewish time, I drop in at the synagogue mere blocks from my house most regularly in late December, the occasion of my father's Yarzheit.

But if I think I've authenticated my Jewish self—and mostly, I do—what of my Southern self? What crosses must I still bear? What more signs can I see, before I accept the authentic voice of my inner Southern man?

I've often felt like Quentin Compson in Faulkner's *Absalom, Absalom!*, when he screamed into the steely Cambridge night, "I don't hate the South. I don't hate it!" Yet there have been many times when I was dying to live elsewhere—New York, Seattle, Burlington, VT. I've even made efforts to do so, but job realities, guilt about leaving my parents and my in-laws, and a hard-to-accept general homesickness have kept me tied to this region.

So when my teenage daughter began speaking in a rich Southern drawl and wearing that tiny Jesus cross, the thought of fleeing
the South crossed my mind again. I feared being blamed for a
condition I couldn't help and had directly, but unintentionally,
passed down to her. Everyone can see the beautiful and exotic
Middle-Eastern genes my daughter proudly wears. However, everyone can also hear the stereotyped Southerner in her voice—a
voice that I've tried so hard to stifle in myself ever since my high
school training as a Thespian.

Yes, I do feel "above" such Southernness: Poor grammar; a
tendency to want to fight "just because;" being a hick for George
Wallace; waving an outdated starred and barred banner in a Black
man's face. These were not the signposts of my soul, but they were
the experiences of my life. Once, when I heard my own father
refer to himself as "just another Southern redneck," I couldn't
sleep that night:

"But Dad, you aren't a redneck...I mean, you love pastrami
on rye!"

"Yeah, but I like a good pork barbecue, too."

Well, so do I.

My wife is Iranian, and the only aspect of Southern culture
that she's fully embraced is life in Mayberry on reruns of *The
Andy Griffith Show*, where the town's only fear is Deputy Fife's
one-bullet-loaded gun. Hearing my daughter say "rahce" for
"rice" and "mah" for "my," this otherwise gentle and loving Persian woman turned on me, the source of these particular drawn-
out inflections.

"Can't you do something?!!!!"

Unfortunately, it seemed, I already had.

I couldn't bother about voice, though, when crosses were emblazoned in my sight. So, beholding my daughter's petite golden
icon, I said a brief, silent prayer to the Jewish God I sort of believe
in, waited not-so-calmly until my wife arrived home, and turned
on *her*:

"Oh. Her cross? Well, she's wearing it because it gives her

comfort. She says it makes her feel safer. You know, after that friend of hers was killed in the wreck?"

All I could think then was that my wife, a psychotherapist, always has a ready answer for what I don't understand and probably don't like. Yet here, my most immediate reaction was shame. I didn't realize that my daughter needed that sort of security, or that in her confident outward attitude there lay deeper fears.

"You could ask her about it," my wife psychologized.

Yes, I could.

I'm driving my daughter home from school. She's a precocious second grader, but innocent. I believe too innocent. Just the week before, we developed the set of spring pictures we took of her and her little sister, dressed in white lace gowns that my mother bought for them—ribbons in Pari's hair, a bonnet for her sister Layla. The photos are sepia-toned; the girls are sitting on the front steps of our A-framed yellow house, a safe haven In one shot, Pari is pointing Layla toward the camera, smiling, encouraging her to smile. In another, Pari stands by our blooming white dogwood tree, her plastic blue swing hanging in the background. She stands much older than seven, the look on her face registering the countless poses she's been asked to perform. But she's not exasperated or even resigned. She seems amused, playful. She knows she's indulging Mom and Dad who want to record her every childhood second.

When I see this picture, she looks for all the world like Anne Frank—that picture of Anne adorning most paperback covers of her Diary, a slight darkness under her eyes, but smiling nevertheless, at what, we'll never know.

I think: My little Jewish girl, though I'm not sure of the extent of my own Jewishness, much less the amount I want to impose on her. There is my pride and joy...but also my fear. To see Anne Frank in my daughter's eyes also scares me, so I keep the image deep within. For my heart only.

"Daddy! She calls me back to the drive home. "In school today Evan begged me to start going to church."

"He did what? I was trying so hard to keep the fear and outrage out of my voice. Evan was one of her best friends; it was a moment to walk softly through.

"He said that he didn't want me to go to hell when I died, so would I PLEASE start going to church with him."

"What did you say to him?"

"I said I'm not going to hell, don't worry about it Evan."

"And?"

"He said OK, but that he was going to pray for me."

"And how do you feel about that?"

"It's all right if he wants to. I don't mind. But Daddy?"

"Yes?"

"I don't want to go to church."

"Oh sweetie, we don't have any plans to go to church."

"OK, what's for supper?"

As I reflected on our past, I wondered if I could really ask about her cross without seeming to judge her at the same time, without seeming to undermine the confidence she has in herself... and in me.

I might have swallowed my daughter's choice without choking had it not been for the Star of David pendant I gave her five years earlier, a pseudo Bat Mitzvah present. OK, maybe I forced it on her. I *told* myself that she wanted it, and of course, I wanted to please her. I also wanted to show our world my own pride in the Jewish daughter I was raising. She would *be* what I never had the chance to be: A secure, Southern Jewish *child*. And in fact she did wear it with pride for a few weeks.

Then she admitted that her excitement at receiving it was not as great as she pretended.

She was simply trying to please me.

She confessed that her deeper fears lay in how I would perceive her if she didn't want to wear it, how she might disappoint me when she couldn't be all that I wanted her to be. But that confession came after she removed the star—after she had been urged to remove it by my wife's sister in a letter that my daughter shared with me:

"Take it off, please, for my sake," my sister-in-law's letter ran.

For her sake? When did the wishes of a maternal aunt begin outweighing the gifts of a father?

Through the years my wife and I have been married, I've come to realize this: My wife's oldest sister was a more present maternal influence on my wife than their mother had ever been. And this maternal instinct reached deep within all of us: A protective impulse, sincere, caring, yet occasionally overstepping. My sister-in-law's fear: Was it safe for our child to proudly and publicly declare that she is Jewish? Especially in the South? For this woman knows first-hand the experience of persecution. She lived in Khomeini's Iran. She knows what we native Southerners all know, whether we choose to admit it or not: Tolerance of minorities in this region is tenuous, highly temporal, and maybe always will be. To stand out might not kill you, but....

So is proclaiming that you're one with the tribe that not so long ago was openly called "Christ-Killers" worth the risk of fatherly pride?

Not for my sister-in-law, and certainly not, in her view, for her niece.

But I didn't want to see her view. I had been wronged, second-guessed, reprimanded, and shown up in front of my daughter. I saw myself as one with my father, other oppressed Southern Jews, Holocaust victims, marranos—Jewish scapegoats all the way back to Moses and Abraham. All wronged for no other reason than for whom they were. Would I allow that to happen to me? Wouldn't I proudly wear a Star and pass one down to my daughter, risking safety for identity's sake?

It turned out that the answer to these questions was "NO." I yielded to the borne-cross of my fear and to the wisdom of those who had contended with their own. For I heard this truth at least: In wanting my daughter to wear her Jewish pride, I hadn't considered what that pride might put her through in small-town, public school-ville South Carolina.

After weeks of simmering righteousness, my sister-in-law and I settled our differences. She cried about her fear, her transgression into our nuclear world. I apologized for my harsh words—words that today I hope neither of us remembers. We hugged that day, on the grounds of Snowbird Lodge, the specially-designated site for our truce. Still, Southern man that I am, I held onto my grudge and my fears for years after, believing I had lost the war for my daughter's identity and oddly enjoying my own victimhood:

The fiery red cross of my own choosing.

So when I told Pari that she didn't have to wear the Star, especially if she were only doing so to please me, I saw her relief as she removed it and placed it in her jewelry box.

"I'll always keep it, Daddy!"

I wasn't satisfied, but I thought I could accept the conditions.

Until I saw the Cross.

I waited two years before I asked about it, both fearing and desiring her truth. I never really believed that she had gone Christian on me. I knew her better than that, though a real part of me also believed that she was leaving me behind. Of course, when I finally asked her about this tiny, slivered emblem, I learned that there was more Southern culture to this story than I had imagined.

II

As a doctoral candidate in the mid-1980's concentrating on 20th Century fiction, I began pursuing Southern Literature in earnest. William Faulkner and Flannery O'Connor touched and provoked my Alabama soul. O'Connor proclaimed the South a "Christ-haunted landscape." Its crosses beckoned from wooded roadsides and from downtown stores, competing with preachers shouting their holiness from atop their rusted-over cars. These signs of the Southern gothic world appealed to me in that strangely perverse way of recognizing that what scares you the most is also what most fascinates you too.

This was my agnostic period, and I got there naturally and logically. Well, emotionally too. I had been told by a college acquaintance that I was going to hell because I didn't believe in hell. But my mother, a devout Southern Christian, doesn't believe in it either. I couldn't reconcile notions of a loving "personal savior" with a harsh God who, as many of my church peers and teachers believed, would consign anyone but practicing Christians to a fiery hell. What about my father? Would God send him to hell?

When I was ten, one of my Sunday school teachers tried to help:

"Most Jews accept Jesus as the savior today."

When I repeated this to my mother, exuberant in my own relief from this most basic fear, she merely rolled her eyes and said,

"Don't believe everything you hear. Some people think they know everything!"

So, unable to reconcile what I didn't want to look at so closely anyway, I eventually exchanged the *Bible* for the secular literature and culture of the Bible Belt.

Graduate school changed my life in more ways than you can prepare a good Southern barbecue. It was the early 1980's. Southern Punk and New Wave bands like REM and The B-52's thankfully replaced Southern Rock bands like Charlie Daniels and my favorite Shibboleth, Lynyrd Skynyrd, in my consciousness. I particularly hated Skynyrd's hit, "Sweet Home Alabama," as it so clearly dismissed one of my favorite rock idols, Neil Young, who had had the audacity to complain about the South's atrocious racial history in several of his own songs. As Young predicted, the "Southern Man's...crosses were burnin' fast." But not fast enough for me.

For the landscape around me *was* Christ-obsessed, and I

couldn't combat it with just REM and O'Connor's "Hazel Motes" and his "Church of Christ Crucified, Without Christ." With three highly-steepled churches hovering just beyond my grad school bedroom window, it simply wasn't possible to ignore Jesus or his symbols.

But it was possible to turn to my father's Jewish faith.

I began making that turn when I interviewed for the job I've held for the past twenty-five years: A professorship at a small, church-related liberal arts college in rural South Carolina. After a very positive initial interview, a member of the college's English Department—someone I had never spoken to in my life— called me one day as I sat in my office.

"Oh, hello Terry, I'm so glad you're interested in joining us. I've heard such wonderful things about you from the committee! But, there's one thing they forgot to ask: Are you a member of a Christian church?"

"Uhhhhhh, er, yes, I was raised in a Methodist church."

"Really, oh that's so wonderful! Well that's all I need to know. I hope we get to meet soon!"

And that was it. The entire conversation lasted three minutes. I walked up and down the floor of my office afterward, asking any and all I saw exactly what they thought this question meant. I was sure I had given them the "right" answer, but I was less sure what the question and answer meant to me.

As it turned out, that was the day, in my soul at least, that I became a Jew.

Since then I have published scholarly articles on Jewish family meals in film and TV; on the role my father's rabbi played in Birmingham's civil rights era; on Jewish gangsters. I have taught courses in the Literature of the Holocaust, the Jewish Literary Renaissance, and even a course in Southern Jewish Literature. I am a secular and scholarly Southern Jewish man, and I am the college's first avowed Jewish faculty member. I have tenure, am a full professor, and was the 2010–11 Professor of the Year.

Yet I have faced these trials.

Once, in my Literature of the Holocaust class, a young woman spoke up during a discussion of Primo Levi's Holocaust memoir, *Survival in Auschwitz*:

"It breaks my heart that these poor Jewish victims are still going to hell. I just feel so bad for them."

Another young woman, wearing a beautiful gold cross tied around her neck, tried to witness to me after that class.

She sat in front of my desk, in the chair I provided for her.

"I hear you talk about all those who lost faith during the Holocaust and of others whose beliefs weren't strong enough to save themselves or anyone else. So what faith do believe?"

"That's what I believe." And I pointed to the COEXIST poster on my wall. In the word, the "C" is a Moslem crescent; the "X" is a Jewish star, and the "T" is a cross.

She continued looking at me, and I wasn't sure if I was reading confusion, disbelief, pity, or something else in her face. Finally, she just shook her head and strode out the door. A few months later she sent me a letter asking if I'd donate money for her mission trip to Africa where she would be spreading the Word to the poor masses there. I politely declined.

And then, during the college's most intense time of debating our Christians-only hiring policy—a time when everyone who knew me knew I was Jewish—I was asked to join a group of faculty and students for a forum at the college's Winter Conference, a religious retreat. The forum was composed of two faculty members from the Religion Department, an untenured but very popular History professor, and me.

The retreat took place in a former YMCA camp, high in the southern Appalachian Mountains. The lodge felt like my old Sunday school classes: A lot of knotty pine, sweet disinfectant odors, and sincere and earnest people, though clearly, not many who wanted to hear questions and doubts. We sat in a semi-circle that night, I on one end, our most senior Religion professor on the other. Students and faculty spouses—my own wife and daughters included—made up the audience. My memory now says we were all lit by candles, thousands of candle-lights amidst the shadows of winter night hovering just beyond the row of windows behind us.

And with Jesus hanging above us.

I remember at one moment my Religion colleague declared,

"All I know is that Jesus said that the only path to eternal life was through Him." I stared out at my wife who looked back at me. At least *she* met my eyes.

I wondered then: If I looked above me, exactly whose image would now be hanging there?

I told the assembled students and families my story and asked this question:

"How could I ever make such a narrow, limiting choice— Christian *or* Jew; heaven *or* hell—when my parents were from different faiths? Elie Wiesel had to choose to leave his father behind in a camp in order to survive, but I can't make a choice that, according to many of you, would separate me eternally from my father."

"But faith in Jesus is a gift," one enthusiastic student answered.

"How would you respond," I asked him, "if you extended that gift to someone, and he very politely said 'No thanks?'"

"I'd just pity him," the student said.

"He may not want, need, or think he has done anything to deserve your pity," I said. The room grew very quiet then.

Later that night a Christian rock band was preparing to lead everyone in "Praise" music. That same student, the band's lead guitarist, wearing a large wooden cross attached to a naugahyde cord around his neck, began warming up with his mates. Standing there, I was proud of myself, the stance I had taken. But I was also not sure of the crowd I was in the midst of. Who there thought I was going to hell with my father, most likely dragging my wife and daughters behind? Mulling over my mixed-up reality, I heard the warm-up grow rowdier, and all of a sudden, the guitarist broke into the opening bars of "Sweet Home Alabama." I felt like running away from this peculiar cross, or yelling "Roll Tide," the battle cry of my beloved Alabama Crimson

Tide. Instead, I stayed and listened.

III

In the two years I contemplated silently my daughter's cross, I began wondering whether I *could* learn to love the Christ-haunted landscape of my home region. After all, my own father did. He and his Jewish cousins worked their lives in a wholesale jewelry store. How many times did he praise to me, as if I truly cared about the merchandise I had to box up during my years of summer employment there, the store's best-selling items?

Crosses and Crucifixes.

"We have to please the customers. They're always right," he'd say.

Neither did it seem to bother him that I was raised in my mother's church, with the sacred icons and portraits of a smiling, bearded savior.

But part of me wished it had.

Can I find the peace of my convictions? Can I accept what I don't understand?

Can I be a Jew and raise a Christian daughter?

These were the questions haunting me after I thought I had accepted my wife's version of my daughter's cross. But there I sat one Thursday night in family therapy staring at the symbol of my heartache. In my wonder and confusion, I heard myself blurt out:

"Could you tell me, sweetie, why you wear that cross, what it means to you?"

She grinned, a bit sheepishly I thought, but looked at me squarely and said, "Do you want to know the real story?"

And from the twinkle in her eyes and the lightness of her smile, I knew that I did— that I'd always want to know her truth.

"Actually, I just told my boyfriend too. He kept wondering why I wore it since he knew that none of us was religious. It kind of worried him. Well...it's all because of that Brad Paisley song."

"That what?"

"That Brad Paisley song, 'She's Everything.'"

I knew who Brad Paisley was. He was part of that genre of

Southern music that I refuse to listen to and that I lament that both of my daughters love, New Country. The affected nasal twang, the purported love of God and Country, the gushing, maudlin sentimentality in every song. The utter simplicity in a world that is anything but simple.

I'm sure Flannery O'Connor would have hated this gushy crap too.

Maybe it's simply that, as my Dad used to say about my music, "It all sounds the same to me." But I hate it. I really do. I hate George Strait, Tricia Yearwood, Toby Keith, Trace Atkins, Rascal Flatts. Perhaps my hatred started the day that my favorite Birmingham FM underground rock station—where, by the way, I had first heard Neil Young's soothing falsetto—changed to a "New Country" format. New Country, to me, is nothing but simplistic, Redneck Southern songs for like-minded listeners, representative of the worst of Southern culture. I can't stand that my daughters like this stuff; I can't stand for anyone to think that my girls are simple, or rednecks. I think I've somehow failed them if I haven't been able to instill in them the knowledge that music, culture, literature, the South itself, are complex, and often dark, realities. That they need to appreciate the reality, the darkness, and the beauty in the midst of it all.

And then it hit me: Have *I* ever really appreciated the complexities of my Southern home?

So I asked my lovely daughter, "What's so great about that song?"

"Well, in it he mentions 'the church girl' who wears 'a cross around her neck,' and I love that song. When I first heard it, I wanted to be that girl. So I asked Mommy to buy a cross for me. It's a silly high school thing, I know, but that's why I wanted it and why I still like it. I want to be someone's 'Everything.'"

Icons resonate in so many ways. I had made my daughter's gesture so complex, but to her, it was a very simple thing.

She laughed then, and her mother, sister, and I joined in. Our therapist said, as he regularly does, "Y'all are a beautiful family.

I love you guys."

And I ask you, how could he not?

Later that night I Googled the complete lyrics to the song:

"She's a warm conversation
That I wouldn't miss for nothing
She's a fighter when she's mad
And she's a lover when she's loving
And she's everything I ever wanted
And everything I need…"

She is my daughter, and, as I learned for the millioneth time deep in my soul, she is someone's "Everything."

I just hope she knows it.

Six years ago, the autumn of 2009, I took Pari to her first Alabama football game, a tradition that my Southern Jewish father held more dearly than any religious holiday. Not an outstanding matchup—Bama versus Tennessee-Chattanooga—but the atmosphere was electric, and she was thrilled to be there—as much to be there with me, I believe, as to see the Tide Roll. Maybe ten, or a hundred times that afternoon, the stadium DJ piped "Sweet Home Alabama" over the Jumbotron airwaves. The first time or two Pari saw me wince.

"What's the matter Dad, don't you love that song?"

I tried telling her about Skynyrd and Neil Young, about Crosses and Stars.

About being a boy raised in the South, scared of shadowy icons he didn't understand.

She just rolled her eyes at me: "Oh Daddy, who cares about that anymore? Nothing can hurt us. It's all fun now!" And she kept on dancing in her place.

And that December, we sat in our den watching Alabama

annihilate Florida and Christian star Tim Tebow for the SEC championship: Pari, my younger daughter Layla, my wife Nilly, our great Bama friend John—a man my age—and me. As the final seconds ticked off the scoreboard clock, Pari jumped up, hooked her IPod to its docking station, and cranked up Skynyrd.

"Turn it up louder," John said.

So she did. "C'mon Daddy, let's dance!"

Forgive me Neil, I couldn't help it. We danced, all of us, as hard as we could. When "Sweet Home" ended, we played it again, louder, and danced even harder. Again and again.

Thanks to my cross-wearing daughter, I've finally seen that not all signs are meant for me, that crosses are not always red, and that my stars will always be there, scattered in the night sky and glittering over me in Bessemer or Greenville. Or wherever I am.

About the Author

TERRY BARR is a Professor of Modern Literature and Creative Writing at Presbyterian College in upstate South Carolina. His essays have been widely published in print and online in such journals as *The Bitter Southerner, Hippocampus, Deep South Magazine, Blue Lyra Review, Blue Bonnet Review, Steel Toe Review,* and *Red Truck Review.* He lives in Greenville, SC, with his wife, two daughters, and their beloved pets, Morgan and Max (the Carolina Wild Dog).